Driving Your Company's Value:
Strategic Benchmarking for Value

Driving Your Company's Value:
Strategic Benchmarking for Value

MICHAEL J. MARD
ROBERT R. DUNNE
EDI OSBORNE
JAMES S. RIGBY, Jr.

WILEY

John Wiley & Sons, Inc.

Library of Congress Cataloging-in-Publication Data:
Driving your company's value : strategic benchmarking for value / Michael J.
Mard ... [et al.].
p.   cm.
Includes index.
ISBN 0-471-64855-8 (cloth)
1. Benchmarking (Management)   2. Economic value added.   3. Strategic
planning.   I. Mard, Michael J.
HD62.15.D74 2005
658.4′013—dc22   2004021371

HD
62.15
.D74
2004

To Seph—Go UCF and 3 Plates. We love you.

—*Mike Mard*

I wish to express my appreciation to the members of the Consulting Accountants' RoundTable for all their support and inspiration over the years; your ideas and demands for better tools contributed greatly to the methodologies and body of work we teach. To my family, thank you for all your patience with my schedule and encouragement to "go for it." To my life and work partner, Steve, I dedicate this effort in appreciation for your intellectual and absolute support to everything I undertake.

—*Edi Osborne*

To Susan and Maryanne.

—*Jim Rigby*

To Linda and Sean.

—*Bob Dunne*

About the Authors

Robert R. Dunne, Master of Science in Management and Strategic Studies, is President of KnowledgeLeaders, Inc., a not-for-profit organization serving to advance the development and management of intellectual capital. He served 26 years in the U.S. Navy and completed his military career as a captain (O-6). As a graduate school professor he taught senior, civilian, and military executives, from around the world, how to formulate, align, resource, and execute strategy. Mr. Dunne has facilitated the development and implementation of hundreds of strategy-aligned campaigns that have documented millions in revenue increases and cost savings. He is an internationally recognized speaker on strategy execution.

Michael J. Mard, CPA/ABV, ASA, is a Managing Director of The Financial Valuation Group (FVG) in Tampa, Florida. He was founding president of The Financial Consulting Group, a national association of professional service firms dedicated to excellence in valuation, litigation, and financial consulting. Mr. Mard has been a full-time business appraiser and expert witness for over 19 years. He is author of *Valuation for Financial Reporting: Intangible Assets, Goodwill, and Impairment Analysis, SFAS 141 and 142*, contributing author of *Financial Valuation: Applications and Models* and *coauthor of Financial Valuation Workbook*, all published by John Wiley & Sons, Inc. Mr. Mard has coauthored over 20 courses and published over 60 articles. He has been a presenter, speaker, and instructor more than 70 times.

Edi Osborne, CSPM, CPBA, is CEO of Mentor Plus in Pleasanton, California. Ms. Osborne is coauthor and primary facilitator/trainer of The Profit Equation[SM] seminar and Performance Measurement PLUS Skills and Systems Workshop offered in cooperation with the American Institute of Certified Public Accountants (AICPA). Ms. Osborne is also coauthor of the *Strategic Performance Management* credential program. As a nationally recognized public speaker, she has spoken at many conferences sponsored by the AICPA, state societies, and international associations. She has been published in *Accounting Today* and the *Journal of Accountancy*. She has conducted client and team advisory boards and team/client training programs as well as strategic planning processes for over 100 accounting firms. In addition to facilitating business development roundtables for business owners throughout the state of California, Ms. Osborne developed the Group Mentoring program at San Jose State University's Center to Develop Women Entrepreneurs.

James S. Rigby, Jr., CPA/ABV, ASA, is a Managing Director of The Financial Valuation Group (FVG) and current President of the Financial Consulting Group. Mr. Rigby has over 25 years of professional experience. He has provided consulting services related to strategic planning, international expansions, mergers and acquisitions, and intellectual property; and expert testimony related to valuations. Mr. Rigby has served on various business valuation/litigation committees of the AICPA, American Society of Appraisers (ASA), and other professional associations. He is the coauthor of multiple continuing education courses and articles published in a variety of professional journals.

Contents

Preface

This book is about value metrics within strategy execution. In today's knowledge-based economy, senior executives are faced with the challenge of optimizing their investment in systems and human capital to help their business:

- Execute strategy
- Improve productivity
- Enhance the perceived value of its own products and services

To capture the full value of an organization it is essential to closely align strategic planning and operational execution. The Strategic Benchmarking for Value (SBfV) Model does just that. The model identifies three key elements—strategy, systems, and people—that need to be managed synchronously to derive full value from all three factors (see Exhibit A). It provides a systematic way of planning and monitoring a successful business strategy with the necessary systems and people infrastructures to execute it. It provides a practical and powerful way to ensure that businesses get the full benefit from their investment in systems and people. It is a means of giving order with clarity to the process of bringing an organization's business plan and budget into unity with the infrastructure to make the plan work. Only when a business's strategy, systems, and people have been aligned can the business advance successfully.

Today's enlightened leaders understand that a focus on value creation is a holistic endeavor and cannot be accomplished by simply focusing on individual pieces of the value creation process. A holistic approach to the value creation process requires:

- A consistent approach to management planning, resource allocation, performance assessment, and communication.
- A management focus on and priority of value creation.
- Alignment of management action with strategic objectives and shareholder value.
- An understanding of the Five Dimensions of the value creation process.
- Strategic benchmarking to monitor the value creation process.

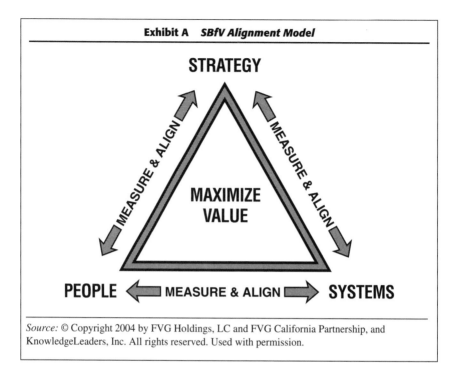

Exhibit A *SBfV Alignment Model*

Organizations seem to find it difficult or impossible to harness the synergy of people and systems for their long-term benefit. The problem is that too much attention is placed on systems or people independent of their links and leverage effects on other business operations, customer value propositions, and each other. Companies fail to recognize the importance of building organizational structures, sets of business processes, and product or service offerings that reflect the interdependence of enterprise strategy, systems' capabilities, and people's skill sets that yield the core competencies to sustain long-term growth and productivity.

SBfV is a powerful, but simple model. It recognizes that different people in an organization make, at different times, different sets of business decisions. The alignment process emphasizes that the decisions need to be coordinated to achieve maximum value.

Acknowledgments

Many people provided comfort and support through our arduous two year effort to bring "Driving Your Company's Value: Strategic Benchmarking for Value" to life. Among others, we thank and are indebted to those that shared their materials with us:

James R. Hitchner, CPA/ABV, ASA and John Wiley & Sons, Inc., for allowing us to use excerpts from *Financial Valuation: Applications and Models*, edited by James R. Hitchner (John Wiley & Sons, Inc.: New Jersey, 2003). Reprinted with permission.

Chuck Kremer and Ron Rizzuto with John Case, for the guidance of Managing by the Numbers, (Cambridge, MA: Perseus Publishing, 2000).

The American Institute of Certified Public Accountants (AICPA). Portions of various documents, copyrighted by the AICPA, Harborside Financial Center, 201 Plaza Three, Jersey City, NJ 07311-3881 are reprinted with permission.

Dr. Sheila Kessler, for allowing us to use your list of Critical Success Factors.

Warren Miller, Beckmill Research, for allowing us to use your Airline Industry Analysis; as well as sharing the concepts on performance ratios in your presentation to the Financial Consulting Group.

Chris Mobley, Mobley Matrix International, Inc., and Chuck Kremer for allowing the use of the Mobley Matrix.

We thank many reviewers who slogged through the very rough original manuscript and provided patient and detailed suggestions for improvement:

William Braun, CPA, MBA, MIM, Decision Point Solutions, LLC

James Hitchner, CPA/ABV, ASA, The Financial Valuation Group

Jay Jamrog, Executive Director, Human Resources Institute

Joseph E. McCann, III, Ph.D. University of Tampa

Richard J. Monsma, CPA, The Copeland Group

Rick E. Norris, JD, CPA, Decision Point Solutions, LLC

Last but far from least, we thank the Tampa staff of The Financial Valuation Group. Without you this book would have remained a concept on a napkin:

Deanna Muraki deserves our special thanks for overseeing and coordinating this entire effort and for expertly bringing the work of four authors together into one. Her weekly reminders and hours of organization kept us moving forward through numerous edits and revisions.

To *Faye Danger*, our thanks for her encouragement and assistance in the editing process. This support kept us focused as we journeyed through this project.

To *Kelly Rowjohn*, our thanks for her editorial assistance from the development process through completion of this book. Her editorial insights and persistence in obtaining permission to reprint important material have been vital in bringing this book to press.

All of these friends and colleagues get much deserved credit for all that was done right in this book. For all that was done wrong, we authors can only look in our collective mirrors and accept full responsibility.

Overview

The goal of today's owners and managers is to be able to continually drive their company's value higher. As a result, consultants constantly present these business owners, executives, and investors with the hottest new idea for business management success. Every few years, someone comes along with another fad to be promoted to company management in order to sell books or professional consulting services. Between all of these fads, the business community always comes back to the basic concept that good management is the key to success. Enlightened leaders understand that enterprise value is created by business strategy based on the company's critical success factors being effectively executed.

In today's knowledge-based economy, management's responsibility is to develop a strategy that optimizes their investment in the company's tangible and intangible assets. To ensure that the strategy is executed effectively, the company needs a benchmarking system to monitor the effectiveness of the strategy and to identify necessary modifications to the strategy to enhance the value creation process. An appropriate benchmarking or monitoring system will also identify failures in the execution that would eventually diminish the value of the company. Management must be able to drive the company's value by enhancing productivity derived from a strategy effectively executed through the company's people and systems.

Many studies have been made of successful companies by looking at their financial ratios, management philosophies, intangible assets, or any other factor the researchers believe may have affected the company's success and ability to outperform other companies. These insights are helpful but most often they provide abstract concepts to be adapted to the individual company.

Institutional and other investors in public companies consider certain characteristics of companies to be more important than others in creating value for the stockholders. An Ernst and Young (E&Y) study, titled *Measures That Matter*,[1] of investors and investment managers concluded the following characteristics are considered the most important for creating shareholder value. Thirty-nine individual factors were ranked in importance by the investors and grouped into eight categories by E&Y. The weighted average of each factor's ranking (factors were ranked from 1 to 39) determined the importance of each value-creating characteristic or category grouping. The characteristics are listed below in their order of importance:

1. Quality of management
2. Strength of market position
3. Effectiveness of new product development
4. Effectiveness of the executive compensation policies
5. Level of customer satisfaction
6. Quality of investor communications
7. Quality of products and services
8. Strength of corporate culture

While a lot of interpretations can be made from the underlying 39 factors that were ranked by the investors and grouped into these eight categories, four observations are extremely important for management and owners to remember:

- The quality of the company's products and services is *not* very high on the list.
- The company's market position is second on the list. This reflects the attitude of Jack Welch, former CEO of General Electric, who was often quoted as saying that he did not want to be in a business if he could not be the number one– or two–ranked competitor.
- The strength of the corporate culture, normally associated with employee satisfaction, is at the bottom of the list. While this investment attitude may be correct for large public companies, we believe for small to midsized businesses, corporate culture and employee satisfaction would be ranked much higher on the list of items creating company value in the eyes of investors and owners.
- The fourth ranked characteristic, "effectiveness of executive compensation policies," would move to the top position in importance if one of the other factors were reclassified. We believe that the factor "ratio of CEO compensation to workforce compensation" is related more to corporate culture and employee satisfaction than it is to the "effectiveness of executive compensation systems." With this modification in the grouping of factors, the "effectiveness of executive compensation systems" item would have an average factor ranking that would place it in the number one position.

Our conclusions from reading this study's results are that:

- Investors consider quality of management as the most important company characteristic for creating value because they believe management can affect the other characteristics of the company through good management and an effectively executed strategy.

- Executive compensation focused on performance and alignment with shareholder interests will motivate and direct management's efforts.
- Market position reflects customer satisfaction and the idea that the company is producing or providing products or services at a level acceptable to its customers. Therefore, the quality of the products or services themselves, as compared to competitors', is not as important as the customer's belief that the products meet his or her expectations for that particular product or service.
- Effective new product development capabilities are necessary to ensure the continued success and growth of the company. Without new products the company cannot have continued revenue growth or stay current with technological advances of its competitors.

Another study was completed by PricewaterhouseCoopers (PwC) in 2003, titled "Out–Performance: Delivering Better Returns Over the Long Term."[2] The executive summary identifies two characteristics of high-performing companies that are applicable to companies of all sizes:

- **A focus on strategy**—Outperformers used value drivers (critical success factors) to focus employees' efforts.
- **An enhanced understanding of risk and value**—Outperformers were significantly more likely to manage for value. They had an understanding of their financial and industry success factors that minimized the risks associated with their particular business strategies.

Creating maximum value for the owners is accomplished only when management focuses its activities on the most important success factors of the business. Therefore, management must determine its business strategy, identify the critical success factors for that strategy, identify the key performance indicators related to those critical success factors, and establish performance benchmarks for the key performance indicators. Only by focusing management's limited time and the company's limited resources on the critical success factors can management create maximum value for the shareholders.

Identifying what creates value in a particular company is becoming extremely important to management because stockholders and boards of directors are increasingly aware that:

- Traditional accounting measures are not reliably linked to shareholder value.
- The company's assets are often undermanaged.

- Management's actions and rewards need to be aligned for long-term value creation.
- The media is publicizing the need for, and ranking companies on, their value creation.

UNDERSTANDING VALUE

In order to understand the value creation process, management must understand value and the basic variables that create value. Value has been historically and correctly defined by the mathematical formula of:

$$\text{Value} = \frac{I}{R-G}$$

I = Income
R = Risk
G = Growth

or

$$\text{Value} = \frac{\text{Free cash flow (FCF)}}{\text{Cost of capital (CofC)} - \text{Growth in FCF}}$$

As can be seen from the formula, there are only three alternatives available to management to increase stockholder value. Management can:

- Increase the free cash flow available to the stockholders.
- Lower the cost of capital for the company by lowering its business or financial risks.
- Increase the growth rate of the free cash flow available to the stockholders.

FREE CASH FLOW

Free cash flow is the cash that is available to the company's owners after all the company's internal needs have been met.[3] This includes cash for capital expenditures and repayment of debt, and funds for expansion of the company's operating assets such as inventories and accounts receivable.

The company's free cash flow is computed as follows:

Start with:	Net income
Plus:	Depreciation, amortization, and other noncash charges
Less:	Incremental working capital needs

Less:	Incremental capital expenditure needs
Plus:	New debt principal in
Less:	Repayment of debt principal
Equals:	Free cash flow to equity

Management should be constantly monitoring the current free cash flow and the projected free cash flow to ensure that decisions do not negatively affect the company's free cash flow. Short-term drops in free cash flow would be considered only when the present value of the future cash flow has increased sufficiently to warrant the temporary, near-term drop in cash flow.

The value formula discussed previously uses the company's cost of capital (risk rate) as the denominator. For public companies, the cost of equity is reflected in its stock price, while the cost of debt is the interest rate required by its lenders.

For private companies, the equity cost of capital cannot be computed precisely because the company does not have a public stock price. Because the determination of precise value for private companies is difficult, an alternative is needed for management to drive value. We believe that changes in a private company's accounting return on equity (ROE) are an effective proxy for monitoring whether its cost of capital is increasing or decreasing.

Although it is necessary to compute an estimate of the company's cost of equity to determine its value, it is not necessary to estimate the cost of equity to determine if the company is increasing its value by, say, decreasing its overall risk or cost of capital. Management should be primarily concerned with continually increasing the company's value, not in constantly monitoring the actual value of the company. Having said that, it is natural (and frequently done) that management and owners have a tendency to focus more on the actual value of the company at any one time than on the process of creating value.

When management uses the ROE as a proxy for monitoring the change in cost of capital, it must also understand the risk of changes in the company's capital structure. For instance, management must temper its desire to lower financial risk by undertaking more debt if such increases in debt increase the company's business risk of nonpayment to unacceptable levels. Pushing the debt coverage limits and allowing an insufficient margin for error in planning debt coverage will increase the company's business risk and lower its value. As a result, ROE should be managed both historically and on a forecasted basis. Good forecasts will help management understand the effects of its borrowing decisions and the margin for error these decisions allow. Managing the factors that affect the company's free cash flow and ROE will ensure that management's overall decisions are increasing the company's value.

$$\text{VALUE} = \frac{\text{Free cash flow}}{\text{ROE} - \text{Growth in free cash flow}}$$

Return on Equity

Return on equity is important because it monitors the company's:

- Profit on sales
- Effectiveness in the use of its assets (asset turnover)
- Use of leverage or extent of debt financing

The return on equity (ROE) ratio is computed as follows:

$$\text{ROE} = \frac{\text{Net income}}{\text{Shareholder's equity}}$$

Clearly, the ratio itself does not directly show the effects of profitability, turnover, and leverage, but if it is broken down into its component parts via the DuPont Formula, the relationship becomes clear.

$$\text{ROE} = \text{Profitability} \times \text{Turnover} \times \text{Leverage}$$

or

$$\text{ROE} = \frac{\text{Net income}}{\text{Sales}} \times \frac{\text{Sales}}{\text{Total assets}} \times \frac{\text{Total assets}}{\text{Equity}}$$

Apply simple algebra, and everything cancels except net income divided by shareholder's equity.

Rich Gildersleeve in *Winning Business* explains return on equity as follows:

> [T]he more income a company earns from an equity investment, the better. Shareholders like to see very large ROEs. High ROEs typically drive up share prices since the company is efficiently earning money with its equity capital. The relationship between ROE and net income is apparent from the first formula; however, that formula does not appreciably help management decide what to change to improve ROE.
>
> Although the second formula yields the identical result for ROE, it helps the manager more than the first. In the second formula, ROE is

equivalent to profitability multiplied by asset turnover multiplied by financial leverage. By increasing any of these factors, management can enhance ROE.

High ROE values generally indicate good performance although it is important for you to understand the reasons for a higher or lower trending ROE. Higher ROEs may not be desirable if the company must assume too high a risk in its product offering or degree of debt leverage. Higher ROEs indicate that net profit, and/or asset turnover, and/or financial leverage are increasing. Increases in net profit are good to the extent that a company does not sacrifice growth potential, sales levels, and quality. Increases in asset turnover are good to the extent that a company retains sufficient assets to optimize operations efficiencies. Increases in financial leverage can be positive to the extent that the company has not acquired so much debt for the purchase of assets that the company is at risk of default.[4]

THE FIVE DIMENSIONS OF VALUE

Increasing a company's return on equity requires that managers make all strategic decisions focusing on one or more of the Five Dimensions of Value. Every strategic action to create value must correspond to one or more of these Five Dimensions of Value. The Five Dimensions of Value are related to growth and productivity within a company as follows:

Growth Dimensions

- Increase market share using a constant capital investment.
- Invest capital in projects that yield a higher economic return, such as a new product line.

Productivity Dimensions

- Increase profit through operating efficiencies while using a constant capital structure.
- Maintain profit while using less capital through improved asset utilization (turnover).
- Maintain or improve profit while lowering the weighted average cost of capital (WACC).

Management must focus on the Five Dimensions of Value to analyze its strategic initiatives. Every decision should include questioning if the action will accomplish the goals of one or more of the Five Dimensions of Value.

The first of the five dimensions, increasing market share using a constant capital investment, means that long-term, consistent growth in profits can be accomplished only by expanding the company's market share and therefore its revenues. The growth in the size of the marketplace may increase revenues temporarily without the company's obtaining a larger market share, but eventually most markets flatten or decline in size due to many factors such as new technology or changes in consumers' buying habits. Management must continually focus its efforts on increasing market share.

The second of the five dimensions, investing capital in projects that yield a higher economic return, such as a new product line, means simply that a higher profit margin will increase a company's free cash flow. An investment in a new, higher-margin product line will increase cash flow in two ways. First, each dollar of new sales will provide more free cash flow than the older product line. Second, new products will produce additional revenue from an expanded product line reaching a larger market.

The third dimension of value, increasing profit through operating efficiencies while using a constant capital structure, recognizes that profits and the related free cash flow can be increased through operating efficiencies which lower operating costs without requiring investment in new assets. For example, companies can use overtime or a second shift without significant capital expenditure as opposed to building a new factory or a factory addition.

The fourth dimension, maintaining consistent profits while using less capital through improved asset utilization, means that increased efficiencies will lower capital invested in the company and thus create excess assets, which can be distributed to the stockholders either directly or through cash generated by their liquidation. This additional free cash flow can be invested in other activities that will increase the shareholders' total personal returns and total personal net worth without decreasing the value of the company.

The fifth dimension, maintaining or improving profit while lowering the weighted average cost of capital (WACC), recognizes that a company may not be using its available debt (other people's money) appropriately. Cost of capital is the combination of the return that the company is expected to pay its lenders and investors in return for the debt and equity capital it needs to operate the business. Many private companies use little debt, perhaps for fear of the additional business/financial risk. This has the effect of establishing the company's expected returns (its hurdle rate) at the higher equity level. This results in a higher WACC (in the denominator), which lowers value. Utilizing appropriate debt levels that have interest rates lower than the equity return, results in lowering the weighted average of debt and equity (WACC). A lower WACC (in the denominator) increases value. This tactic works in conjunction with the fourth dimension (increased asset utilization) to increase free cash flow. This extra money can be distributed to the stockholders or used to reduce the need for additional cash investments from the stockholders.

Management decisions based on the Five Dimensions of Value will result in a management style that focuses on value creation.

A HOLISTIC APPROACH

Management must understand that a focus on value creation is a holistic endeavor, constantly and consistently applied. It cannot be accomplished by focusing simply on individual pieces of the value creation process. It cannot be done in a three-month or six-month sprint. Effective change necessary to maximize value requires consistent emphasis over perhaps a two- or three-year period. We are talking about embedding a cultural change and that takes time.

A holistic approach to the value creation process requires:

- A consistent approach to management planning, resource allocation, performance assessment, and communication.
- A management focus and priority on value creation.
- Alignment of management action with strategic objectives.
- An understanding of the Five Dimensions of Value used in strategic decision making.

The Strategic Benchmarking for Value (SBfV) Model was developed to aid today's owners and managers in creating and applying a holistic approach to their company's value creation process and to position their company within the value creation continuum by:

- Improving their strategic decision making.
- Providing greater management accountability.
- Requiring a more effective allocation of their company's resources.
- Improving their capital management.
- Aligning performance measurement to critical success factors.
- Providing a common organizational language.

- Establishing a compensation program aligned with strategic objectives identified in the value creation process.
- Developing a corporate structure that understands how daily actions affect value.
- Providing the management team with a more effective and communicable strategic planning process.

SBfV OR EVA

In looking under the hood of four value creation management philosophies (Managing for Value, Shareholder Value Analysis, Value Based Management, and Economic Value Added), we found that they all had one characteristic in common.

All of them analyzed the return on some type of shareholder equity and most of them are variations of the popular Economic Value Added (EVA) analysis techniques developed by the consulting firm Stern Stewart & Co. in the 1980s.[5]

The comparison of the four philosophies based on type of equity, income stream and the result of the analysis is:

Method	Type of Equity	Income Stream	Result
Return on equity (ROE)	Accounting book value	Net income or free cash flow	Ongoing measurement
Accounting EVA	Accounting book value	Net operating profit after tax (NOPAT)	Benchmark*
EVA	Economic book value	Net operating profit after tax (NOPAT)	Benchmark*
Refined EVA	Market equity	Net operating profit after tax (NOPAT)	Benchmark*

---

*A benchmark to determine what is a good or bad investment. Bad investments are defined as investments not generating sufficient income to provide a return in excess of the company's cost of capital.

RETURN ON EQUITY

ROE, as previously discussed, is one of the best-known ratios used in financial analysis. Every first-year accounting student is taught the ROE ratio, but fewer learn why the ratio is so important in monitoring a company's financial health.

In the early 1900s, the DuPont Formula was developed demonstrating that a company's ROE is actually a summary of the company's profitability, turnover and leverage. ROE is perhaps the best reflection of a company's risk assessment available through our current accounting system. For this reason, the SBfV Process relies heavily on ROE. Accordingly, ROE and the DuPont Formula will be used as one of the key strategic benchmarks for monitoring a company's ongoing effectiveness in creating value.

ECONOMIC VALUE ADDED

EVA was developed principally to determine if a subsidiary or project is adding economic value to a company. Economic value is defined as the company or project creating net operating profit after taxes in excess of its cost of capital. As such, EVA becomes a simple benchmark delineating a good investment from a bad investment.

The implication is that if the company is not covering its cost of capital, the investor should sell or liquidate the investment and invest in an alternative investment that will provide a return in excess of the investor's cost of capital. The EVA concept is primarily a portfolio analysis tool determining investments that should be kept or sold. It can be very effective for large companies with various lines of business in determining which to eliminate or replace, but it does not integrate well into a value creation system that takes a company, over time, from its current financial situation to one that provides a return in excess of its cost of capital. Further, EVA ignores the nonfinancial reasons that an investor, in a closely held company, may be willing to temporarily accept a return less than its cost of capital until the financial results can be improved.

The complexity of the EVA model is significant and requires adjustments to the company's balance sheet and income statement. These adjustments include nonrecurring items, nonoperating items, netting current liabilities (noninterest-bearing) against current assets, adjusting and perhaps adding back amortized goodwill, restructuring costs, capitalized R&D, LIFO reserves, and other items. The goal of the EVA analyst is to produce a financial picture that accurately reflects the current picture and ongoing behavior of the company. These adjustments are not new to the financial analysis field; they are done every day by qualified business valuators. The fact remains, however, that the due diligence required for such analysis is significant and certainly not easy.

In contrast, the SBfV Process starts with the company's current information collection capabilities and its accounting system, and then progresses over time to a more complex analysis as the company improves its profitability and financial- and operational-reporting capabilities.

As the starting point, SBfV focuses on the company's free cash flow and its return on equity as a proxy for the risk-growth portion of the value formula. Therefore, when a company is increasing its free cash flow and its ROE, it is creating value.

The SBfV Process guides the company through the process of self-analysis, starting with its current accounting and information systems capabilities. Management is assisted over time in identifying and documenting its business strategy, identifying its critical success factors and related key performance indicators, establishing a strategic benchmarking system, aligning its goals and objectives with its strategic benchmarking analysis, and then monitoring and adjusting the model and business procedures to create value or to create value faster.

THE SBfV PROCESS

The SBfV Process uses an enhanced scorecard framework. The reasons for an enhanced scorecard are to provide a framework that accounts for the differences between public and private companies, such as:

- The lack of access to capital (debt and equity) experienced by private companies when compared to public companies.
- The need for private companies to include planning to acquire or manage their financial and physical capital in the strategic planning process. Public companies and their subsidiaries treat their financial and physical capital as resources that exist automatically but are not yet allocated. This difference in strategy requirements is a result of the public company's relatively easy access to debt and equity capital to provide working capital or purchase factories and equipment.
- The lack of publicly traded share prices to reflect the private company's success in implementing its strategy to create shareholder value.
- The inability of private companies to precisely determine their cost of capital. Without publicly traded share prices, it is difficult for a company to determine its cost of capital.

- The need to develop a system that will start with the information available and grow with the company as it improves its accounting and information systems to provide for data collection of the required information.

The central core of the SBfV Process is the belief that a company can only increase its value through satisfying the customers' perceived or real needs, wants, or desires. Satisfied customers will purchase the company's products and services on a continual basis, providing an ongoing revenue stream to the company, which management can convert into profits, free cash flow, and a return to the investors.

The SBfV Process is built on a conceptual framework (see Exhibit B), which has four levels that start from the bottom of the framework map. The bottom, or fourth, level consists of the *inputs* (tangible and certain intangible assets) the company uses to create its products and services. The third level consists of the *enablers*, or systems (another form of intangible assets) used to convert the inputs into the products and services used by the customers. The second level represents the *outcomes* (products or services, customer relationships, and company image) from the systems. These outcomes through sales are converted into financial results, the first, or top, level of the framework. The top level, referred to as *effectiveness*, represents the *return on strategic effectiveness*, or the increased value created for the benefit of the shareholders or business owners.

In order to systematically increase the company's value, management should go through SBfV's five-step process (see Exhibit C). The Process's steps consist of:

1. Analysis of the current state or condition of the company.
2. The definition of the desired future state of the company and the strategic plan to create that desired state.
3. Development of the strategic benchmarks and programs to reinforce the benchmarking process key to reaching the desired future state.
4. The aligning of the company's strategies, objectives, personnel, compensation programs, and value drivers into a holistic value creation process.
5. Benchmarking the company's performance on a regular basis and monitoring the results as feedback to enable the design of corrective actions to enhance the value creation process.

The first step in the process requires that management gain a complete understanding of the company. This analysis will be based on internal and external information, but in many cases the analysis of the company based on internal

Exhibit B   ROSE Framework

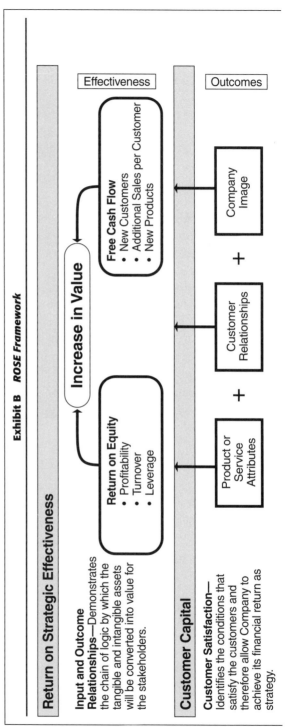

Return on Strategic Effectiveness

Input and Outcome
Relationships—Demonstrates the chain of logic by which the tangible and intangible assets will be converted into value for the stakeholders.

Customer Capital

Customer Satisfaction—
Identifies the conditions that satisfy the customers and therefore allow Company to achieve its financial return as strategy.

Effectiveness

Outcomes

Increase in Value

Return on Equity
- Profitability
- Turnover
- Leverage

Free Cash Flow
- New Customers
- Additional Sales per Customer
- New Products

Product or Service Attributes

+

Customer Relationships

+

Company Image

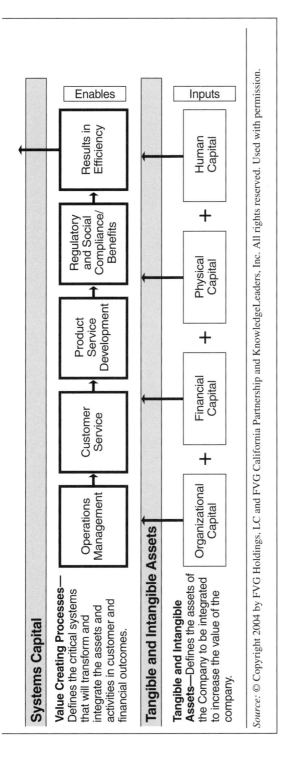

Systems Capital

Value Creating Processes— Defines the critical systems that will transform and integrate the assets and activities in customer and financial outcomes.

Tangible and Intangible Assets

Tangible and Intangible Assets— Defines the assets of the Company to be integrated to increase the value of the company.

Enables

| Operations Management | → | Customer Service | → | Product Service Development | → | Regulatory and Social Compliance/ Benefits | → | Results in Efficiency |

Inputs

Organizational Capital + Financial Capital + Physical Capital + Human Capital

Exhibit C	*The SBfV Five Step Process*
Step	**Objectives**
Step 1 Current State	Data gathering: • Company strategy • Historical financial data • Operational data • Intangible assets and intellectual property data Analysis of current state related to: • Macroeconomic issues • Industry and competitors • Performance areas • Activity measures Review of existing performance measures utilized
Step 2 Desired Future State	Design of future state with respect to: • Core strategy • Core products • Long term business goals • Critical Success Factors • Key Performance Indicators • Benchmarks for measuring strategic effectiveness
Step 3 Strategic Benchmarking Keys	Establish a performance standard (benchmark) for each performance measure utilized Cascade performance measures throughout the organization Secure understanding of contributions of key groups to the value creation process
Step 4 Alignment Execution	Alignment of all Strategy, Systems and People Compensation alignment with strategic benchmarking goals
Step 5 Benchmark and Monitor Return on Strategic Effectiveness (ROSE)	Feedback and milestone checks Focus accountability Measure the Return on Strategic Effectiveness Implementing necessary corrective action Assessing the SBfV Model

financial and operational data will be hampered by a lack of information. Given this, it may become apparent that management will need to improve the quality of the company's information-gathering systems.

Macroeconomic data, industry and competitor information, will need to be gathered and analyzed in light of the company's business strategy and the particular risks associated with that strategy. Identification of the company's current key performance indicators and benchmarks will be the final part of this analysis.

The second step in the Process is documenting management's future desired state of the company. What does management envision the company will look like in five or ten years? This analysis should identify the core business strategy that will be required to achieve the vision for the company. In addition, management should focus on the company's core products, long-term business goals, the critical success factors (CSFs) necessary to carry out the core strategy, and the key performance indicators (KPIs) for each critical success factor.

The third step in the SBfV Process is actually the heart of applying strategic benchmarking throughout the company. Once management has identified the CSFs and the related KPIs, these elements need to be cascaded through various employee levels in the company, and the key employees need to be brought into the long-term value creation process. By establishing activity measures for employee groups that support the KPIs, all employees can be brought into the value creation process.

If management educates the employees about the company's business strategy and their importance in carrying out the strategy, the employees can begin to understand their importance to the company and how their functions help create value. The last part of this step is to establish the benchmarks that should be used for each KPI and related activity measures.

The fourth step in the SBfV Process focuses management's attention on aligning the company's strategy, systems (including assets), and people into an efficient organization where the systems, resources, and people are focused on the right things to carry out the company's business strategy. Part of this step will be to develop a compensation system that is aligned with the company's strategic goals.

The final step in the SBfV Process is to monitor the benchmarks established and to collect feedback related to why the targeted performance level may not have been accomplished. Once problem areas have been identified, the necessary corrective action obviously must be implemented. This feedback and monitoring process is continual and will allow assessment in the SBfV plan developed by the company. Based on this assessment, management can modify the plan to meet the company's ever-changing needs.

The remainder of this book will expand on the SBfV Process's underlying concepts and steps. We believe that any company can benefit from adopting the whole SBfV Process or by working on any one of the steps in the SBfV Process.

NOTES

1. Ernst & Young, "Measures That Matter," E&Y website: *www.ey.com/global/content.nsf/uk/cf_-_library_-_mem.*
2. PricewaterhouseCoopers, "Out-Performance: Delivering Better Returns over the Long Term," PwC website: *www.pwcglobal.com.*
3. Direct to equity cash flow—the authors are not describing the invested capital method for this book.
4. Rich Gildersleeve, *Winning Business: How to Use Financial Analysis and Benchmarks to Outscore Your Competition* (Houston, TX: Cashman Dudley, 1999), p 31.
5. Stern Stewart & Company, "Economic Value Added," Stern Stewart website: *www.sternstewart.com/evaabout/whatis.php.*

STEP 1

Current State

QUALITATIVE ANALYSIS OF THE COMPANY'S CURRENT STATE

To understand the current state of a company, management must look at both its qualitative and quantitative attributes. Historically, management has focused on the quantitative side of the analysis, because the information is verifiable from the company's historical accounting information, which is centered primarily on financial statement numbers and cost accounting numbers. But the qualitative analysis of the company generally provides more insight about the company and its future prospects. This step will focus on some of the common frameworks used to analyze a company, its industry, and its position in the marketplace. Without an understanding of the industry, it is impossible to develop an effective strategy for the company, determine the company's critical success factors, or develop a meaningful performance measurement system designed to create value.

It is a common belief that management should develop its strategies around the company's mission statement. Recently, in a conversation with friends, a statement was made that "a company does not own its mission, rather, the marketplace gives it to you." The conversation continued and the concept was amplified with "a company's mission is to do what it does best better."

Although we often think we set our mission, the marketplace really sets it for us and ultimately determines our success or failure depending on how we respond to the marketplace and its many influences. As management, our responsibility is to read the marketplace, sort of like tea leaves, to determine the company's mission and how we can do what we are doing better than any other company. To accomplish this task management needs to have a complete understanding of the marketplace or industry it operates in.

ANALYZING THE INDUSTRY

There are several frameworks that are often used for looking at the company, the marketplace, and the industry. We will talk about two such frameworks: The Porter Model and the McKinsey & Company's 7-S Model.

The Porter Model

One of the first really structured analyses was presented in a *Harvard Business Review* article by Michael Porter in 1979[1] and expanded on in the early 1980s in his book *Competitive Strategy: Techniques for Analyzing Industries and Competitors.*[2] Porter, a Harvard Business School professor, developed an analytical approach known as The Porter Model by which to analyze and assess company risk associated with industry structure.[3]

Porter divides industry structure into five forces:

1. Rivalry between current incumbents.
2. Threat of new entrants.
3. Bargaining power of customers.
4. Bargaining power of suppliers.
5. The threat of substitute products.[4]

This model, used thoughtfully in a company analysis, can provide valuable information regarding the relative risk to the future market position, growth, and profitability of the subject company.

The following is a simplistic example of the Five Forces analysis of the Porter Model as applied to Ales' Distributing, a beer manufacturer:

Rivalry between current incumbents—The industry is segmented by distributorships affiliated with one or more of the three major domestic manufacturers. As a result, competition between distributorships within a given region or sales territory is intense.

Threat of new entrants—Since all distributorships operate under agreements with one or more of the three dominant domestic manufacturers and are assigned defined sales territories, the threat of new entrants into the marketplace is minimal.

Bargaining power of customers—Due to the intensely competitive nature of the business, customers tend to possess significant bargaining power. Customers in the on-premise segment of the market require high service levels and on-site displays (bar signage, etc.). Off-premise customers also require high service levels, including assistance in product placement and point-of-sale displays to obtain higher product turn, in exchange for greater shelf space.

Bargaining power of suppliers—Distribution agreements with all manufacturers are extremely restrictive. The manufacturer sets product pricing, and distributor inventories are determined by the manufacturer's need to move product, given its short shelf life.

Threat of substitute products—The increased acceptance of premium import products from foreign beer manufacturers poses a potential threat to future unit sales of domestic distributors.

The McKinsey & Company's 7-S Model

A second model for analyzing industry conduct and its impact on a given company is the McKinsey & Company's 7-S framework,[5] which analyzes competitors using seven categories:

1. Strategy
2. Structure
3. Systems
4. Skills
5. Staff
6. Style
7. Superordinate goals[6]

The following is a brief example analyzing Acme Corporation's (a furniture distributor) ability to remain flexible and to adapt to changes in the seven categories:

Strategy—In response to the competitive nature of the industry and profit pressure exerted by the manufacturer by the transferring of certain expenses to distributors, Acme is looking seriously into acquiring neighboring distributorships (wholesaler consolidation), a strategy encouraged by the manufacturer.

Structure—As a sales-focused company, Acme has decentralized the sales process, training its drivers as well as its on-premise and off-premise sales staff to create unique value to the customer by consulting with the customer on product placement, point-of-sale strategy, and inventory management.

Systems—Acme possesses sophisticated sales training systems, including its involvement as a beta test site for the manufacturer's nationwide interactive satellite sales network, making it one of the more technologically advanced distributorships in the wholesaler network.

Skills—Acme possesses the most experienced sales and warehousing staff of any distributor within a 75-mile radius, giving the company an enormous competitive advantage.

Staff—Acme personnel exhibit great pride in their product, to the point of identifying closely with the manufacturer and its national advertising presence, with a deep conviction that they market the finest product in the industry.

Style—Top management exudes teamwork in everything it does, a feeling that pervades the entire organization, resulting in a remarkably cohesive and satisfied workforce.

Superordinate goals—Acme operates on the fundamental principal that is best expressed in its president's motto: "Ensuring our customer's success will ensure our success." The company, therefore, looks beyond the sales mentality to focus on providing value to the customer, which sets it apart from its competitors.

Macroenvironmental Analysis

Further removed from the subject company than industry forces, but still affecting it significantly, are five macroenvironmental sources of risk:

1. Technological risk
2. Sociocultural risk
3. Demographic risk
4. Political risk
5. Global risk[7]

While the company has little or no influence on these risk factors, an assessment of them can be critical in determining the company's (and industry's) future profitability. Shifts in one or more of these risk factors can (and often do) have a material effect on an industry or a company's future fortunes. Therefore, it is prudent for management to perform a thorough analysis of such factors and to, at least once a year, update the analysis.

Analysis of the five macroenvironmental risk factors on the fictional Ale's Distributing reveals:

Technological risk—The company is recognized as a cutting-edge distributor by its competition and its supplier. It has harnessed new technology to track all delivery vehicles at all times, to maximize route organization, and to ensure productivity.

Sociocultural risk—Consumer trends toward premium import products pose a potential risk to the company's product as they gain a stronger foothold in the domestic market.

Demographic risk—The company's territory is composed of three mature counties that possess an aging population with little future growth prospects. Since the company's product is preferred by younger consumers, this is a threat to the company's ability to maintain its past earnings stream.

Political risk—The alcohol industry watched the federal legal action against the tobacco industry with interest, and fears of future regulation or judicial action exist.

Global risk—The three major domestic manufacturers are fighting to make inroads into the global marketplace, with European counterparts looking to the U.S. marketplace to claim market share from existing competitors.

A more expansive example of industry and macroenvironmental analysis was provided by Warren Miller of Beckmill Research (*www.beckmill.com*) (see Exhibit 1.1). This illustration, from the fourth quarter of 2003, was used in a discussion group on strategic planning and covers both the microenvironmental level and the industry level of analysis.

ANALYZING THE COMPANY

The key to analyzing the company's current state is to understand the company itself and how it relates to the industry and the macroenvironment it operates in. To understand the company, management needs to understand many factors about the company including: its business strategy, its development stage, its intangible assets, and its critical success factors (CSF) and the key performance indicators (KPI) related to those CSFs.

Every privately owned company goes through various stages of development to reach maturity. As management must change, the company goes through various stages to react to the environment it operates in. The chart in Exhibit 1.2 shows the three stages of development: infancy, adolescence, and maturity, along with the typical characteristics of the company related to finance, management, operations, marketing, sales, and the owner's personal needs in each stage.

Exhibit 1.1 *Airline Industry Analysis*

Macroenvironmental Analysis for the Airline Industry

1. **Economic**—The recession has buffeted this industry more than most. It is highly cyclical. The effect of downturns is exacerbated by a cost structure that is heavily fixed (see Rivalry). Plummeting interest rates (which reduce the cost of getting new planes) aren't much use when capacity is shrinking, not growing.

2. **Technological**—The Internet has enabled customers (and carriers) to bypass the traditional distribution channel (travel agents, *not* airports). Comparison shopping is now fast and easy through such on-line resources as Expedia, Orbitz (owned by the major airlines themselves), and Travelocity. Proprietary reservation systems (e.g., Sabre), while still useful, are not the big-stick competitive weapons that they used to be because the travel agencies that use them are not the players in this industry that they used to be. In 2002, airlines eliminated most agents' commissions.

   Moreover, advances in satellite communications have enabled newer competitors to change the "passenger experience" by having, as JetBlue does, individual TV monitors for each traveler. In a society that puts enormous value on individual rights, having one's choice of TV channels on a flight is attractive.

   Technology has also made corporate jets more affordable through less expensive design and production methods. Finally, improvements in teleconferencing technology have reduced the need for "face time" between business travelers and those they used to visit.

3. **Sociocultural**—9/11 brought a rebirth of what some have called "traditional values" (family and good friends, especially) in our society. Any industry that makes it tougher to access those values is going to be under a lot of pressure. It's no accident, for instance, that many people who used to think nothing of getting on a plane for a 200- or 300-mile trip now drive or, here on the East Coast, take Amtrak's Acela. The Acela and even driving on take-your-life-in-your-hands I-95 are less stressful than flying. Having a family member on the trip makes tolerable many conditions that aren't when traveling solo.

4. **Demographic**—The demography of the industry has certainly changed. Whereas Southwest used to be almost the sole nontraditional carrier, JetBlue and Airtran (formerly ValuJet) have joined the fray and are building market share. By the end of 2004, JetBlue will have the biggest share in the New York City market. As Wal-Mart did to discount retailing and Dell did to personal-computer assembly, new players in the airline industry bring different views of that industry and how it should work (see Rivalry).

5. **International**—International events have affected the industry. The war in Iraq, unpredictable government policy in Russia (the world's second-largest oil producer after Saudi Arabia), the threat of terrorism in several oil-producing countries, and a surging economy in China have combined to keep fuel prices at all-time highs. Financially weak carriers (United, Delta, Northwest, and to a lesser extent, American) cannot hedge their fuel purchases; cash-flush carriers (e.g., JetBlue) can and do.

   Moreover, security threats from international terrorist organizations created the birth of both the Transportation Security Administration (see below) and the Department of Homeland Security. Those inside the industry will tell you that neither has helped the traditional carriers. Recent horror stories from prominent politicians reinforce the widespread belief that airline security has gone overboard. Both Sen. Edward Kennedy and Rep. John Lewis have reported that they have been kept off commercial flights because there are suspected terrorists with the names "Edward Kennedy" and "John Lewis." Rep. Lewis solved his problem by adding his middle initial, R. Of course, if he can do that, so, presumably, can terrorists.

6. **Political**—The combination of legislative attention (due to federal loans and grants) and new regulatory requirements (principally from the Transportation Security Administration) has

Exhibit 1.1 (Continued)

been especially hard on the large carriers (United, American, and Delta) and, to a lesser extent, the smaller ones (Continental, Northwest, and America West). The bankruptcy filing of United, rumored bankruptcy filings for Delta and US Air (now that Southwest has invaded its Philadelphia hub), and an absence of any public sympathy for the plight of the large carriers have made political help for the industry politically perilous.

Industry Analysis of the Airline Industry

1. **Threat of new entrants**—Barriers to entry which used to be effective deterrents (e.g., switching costs [frequent flyer miles], differentiation [upgrade coupons, access to airline clubs in certain terminals, etc.], capital requirements [when the industry is in the dumper, the price of new aircraft comes down, too, because the market for, say, 767s, 777s, and A320s is limited], *cost advantages independent of scale* [proprietary reservation systems and anticompetitive municipal contracts giving airlines, in effect, ownership of gates at many airports], and *access to distribution channels* [travel agents, an especially lousy business to be in these days unless it's "incentive travel"]) have much less impact these days. Scale economies certainly don't matter when capacity is drastically contracting.

   And if the prohibition against foreign competition between U.S. cities is ever lifted, it will get even uglier.

2. **Rivalry**—The cost structure of the industry is dominated by fixed costs (depreciation, insurance, maintenance). That structure makes for lots of pricing flexibility. But it also means that when demand drops off, margin pressure is extreme, as we have seen since 9/11. The business models of the major carriers have also created "exit barriers" that have exacerbated margin pressure. In the words of one observer, "They won't leave, and they won't change."

3. **Bargaining power of customers** — The passenger angst that has been so much in evidence in the last 24 months really began in the spring of 2000, when the tech sector collapsed. But 9/11 and the recession really brought it home. Most corporations resolutely refuse to pay the $2,000+ fares that used to be routine for walk-ups. Larger firms have "gone direct" to the carriers and insisted on being charged by the mile (with a guarantee of meeting certain travel thresholds, of course).

   Also remember that airline travel is a perishable service from the carriers' point of view. Unlike the house that is not bought today, but can be bought tomorrow, the airline seat that is not sold today can never be sold. So, airline seats are a lot like produce in a grocery store in that they have limited lives and are subject to "spoilage" (hotel rooms are another example). An example: 45 days ago, I priced a go-there-Monday/return-on-Tuesday ticket from BWI to DFW; I didn't find a price under $1,400. Three days ago, I bought the same ticket for $198 (on American).

   Rivalry is also exacerbated by an absurd level of complexity and inefficiency in the systems of the traditional carriers. Unlike Southwest, which flies one kind of plane (Boeing 737s), American, Delta, United, and the rest of the big trunk lines have a multitude of plane models. Many were chosen for specific routes, which makes them difficult to deploy. The complexity increases maintenance, training and inventory costs.

   Then there's the 'us vs. them' [labor vs. management] culture at most of the big carriers. That was highlighted when Don Carty was fired as CEO at American after publicly denouncing rank-and-file employees' reluctance to take voluntary pay cuts, while, at the same time, setting up sweetheart retention contracts for senior executives. Many observe senior executives. Many observers think that retention of experienced airline executives is part of the industry's problem, not part of its solution.

(continues)

Exhibit 1.1 *(Continued)*

The inefficiency and high cost of the industry's hub-and-spoke system of moving passengers to their destinations really pinch when demand is down, and new players who disavow hubs enter and decide to fly point-to-point. The frequent-flyer miles which used to promote brand loyalty are now far less valued than a pleasant flying experience (JetBlue), on-time flights (Southwest), and lower cost (AirTran).

As if that were not enough, there is the mind-numbing complexity of ticket pricing, driven as it is at most big carriers by "yield." On any given domestic flight, there can be as many as 50 different fares, all sitting within a few rows of one another in coach.

Then there is the surly treatment that too many passengers have experienced from airlines that they have flown hundreds of thousands of miles on. One traveler put it this way: "To be hired as an airline pilot, you have to prove you *cannot* tell time. And to be hired as any other airline employee, you have to fail a minimum of five (5) lie-detector tests!"

4. **Bargaining power of suppliers**—This is a good-news/bad-news story for the industry. On the one hand, a weak industry strengthens the hand of incumbents in their dealings with key supplier groups (aircraft manufacturers, labor and fuel providers are three of the most important); but that strength can also be exerted by would-be entrants. In addition, the insurance industry, which used to have to roll over for the airline industry, no longer has to, given the $30 billion bath it took on 9/11 (Warren Buffett's Berkshire Hathaway alone got hit for $3 billion. in cash).

5. **The threat of substitute services**—Substitutes are not the services of head-to-head competitors. They are services that use a different technology to address the same need of the buyer. So, for instance, Amtrak, auto travel, and teleconferencing are increasingly troublesome substitutes for air travel. The existence of substitutes creates pricing ceilings for the service being substituted against. For instance, my wife and I have put a pencil to it: Assuming that everything on a scheduled flight works perfectly, it takes us exactly 15 minutes longer to drive from our home in the Shenandoah Valley of Virginia to Midtown Manhattan than it does to hop a cramped puddle-jumper in Charlottesville, hope to goodness LaGuardia Airport isn't clogged as it so often is, and then endure the white-knuckle cab ride into Midtown by the most indirect route possible. Who needs it?

Source: © Copyright 2004 by Warren Miller, Beckmill Research. Used with permission.

Company's Corporate Strategy

In addition to understanding the company's stage of development, management must understand the company's business strategy. Michael Porter outlined three generic strategies[8] that all businesses must choose from to develop their business strategy. If they do not select one of the strategies, and focus on it over the long term, they will not be effective and will find themselves in the ineffective state he refers to as being "stuck in the middle." The three strategies are:

- Overall cost leadership, (also called Cost Efficiencies *or* Organizational Effectiveness*)*.
- Differentiation from competitors, (also called Product Innovation).

- Focus on a particular buyer group, segment of the product line, or geographic area, (also called Customer Intimacy).[9]

Each of these strategies requires the existence of certain characteristics related to common skills and resources and common organizational requirements. The basic concept is that the resulting strategic position will provide the company with above-average returns in the industry despite having strong competitors. We believe these three strategies are most appropriate for middle-market businesses and thus are core strategies used in Strategic Benchmarking for Value.

Overall Cost Leadership

Pursuing overall cost leadership, or *Cost Efficiencies,* as a strategy requires that management pursue a course of action that:

- Aggressively constructs facilities that are of a scale to have maximum efficiency.
- Focuses on cost reductions gained through experience.
- Includes tight control on costs and overhead.
- Eliminates marginal customer accounts.
- Minimizes costs in areas like service, sales teams, advertising, and research and development.[10]

Even though these companies aggressively work to reduce all costs, they cannot allow their management actions to negatively affect quality, customer service, or new product development.

The Cost Efficiencies strategy's commonly required skills and resources include:

- Continual capital investments and access to capital to fund the investments.
- An engineering team with skills in process engineering.
- High level of labor supervision.
- Designing products for manufacturing simplicity and ease.
- Use of a low-cost distribution system or network.[11]

In addition, the strategy requires the development of many organizational characteristics including:

- The ability to maintain tight cost controls.
- An information infrastructure capable of providing frequent, detailed cost control reports.

Exhibit 1.2 Business Stages of Development Matrix

Finance	Management	Operations	Marketing/Sales	Owner's Personal
Infancy				
Plan and establish:	*Plan and establish:*	*Plan and establish:*	*Plan and establish:*	*Plan and establish:*
Accurate and timely:	Basic goal setting	Production systems	Marketing plan	Personal tax preparation
Bank reconciliation	Vision–mission	Delivery systems	Client/customer	Personal tax planning
Financial statements	development	Workflow mapping	segmentation	Personal financial
A/R and A/P	Core values development	Facilities planning	analysis	planning
Financial literacy	Plan organization	Technology	Identify/target ideal	
training	structure	Space	customer	
Define breakeven	Hiring/recruiting team	Technology installation	Establish contact	
Define income sources	Motivate/educate team	Disaster planning	database	
Technology training	Basic OSHA and HR		Customer service/sales	
Accounting systems	requirements/		Training	
Other	compliance		Systems development	
Tax planning	Compensation planning		Sales protocol	
Tax preparation	Strategic planning		Host beneficiary	
Adolescence				
Develop and document:	*Develop and document:*	*Develop and document:*	*Develop and document:*	*Develop and document:*
Basic flash reporting	HR systems	Quality Control Systems	Pricing analysis	Wills, trusts, etc.
system	Job descriptions	Inventory Control	Feedback systems	Personal financial
Business performance	Procedures manual	Systems	Customer advisory	planning
reviews	Performance reviews	Vendor Relationship	Boards	Estate planning
Budgeting—forecasting	Employee benefit and	Review	Surveys	Retirement planning
Ratio analysis	compensation	Technology review—	Onsite feedback program	Investment planning

28

Banking/financing
Shorten accounting cycle
Trend analysis
Industry comparisons
Cash flow analysis
Accounting systems
    review
Accounting personnel
    recruiting and
    training

planning and analysis
Bonus/incentive programs
Team building activities
Performance standards
    development
Training—Education
Management team
    Development and
    training programs
Develop company I.Q.
    programs

upgrade
Basic CPI monitoring
Quality
Productivity
Utilization
Capacity

Marketing review-ROI
Basic KPI monitoring
Conversion rates
Cost of acquisition
Attrition rate
Lifetime value of a
    Customer
Average
Sale/frequency
Product mix analysis

Formalize Performance Measurement Systems Installation

Maturity

Enhancements:
Advanced financial
    Modeling
Economic value added
Balanced scorecard
    review
Portfolio management
Succession strategy
Activity-based costing
Capital expansion
    Analysis
Advanced financial
    management training
Tracking the life cycle

Enhancements:
Board of directors
    meeting facilities
Retreat facilitation
Equity and profit sharing
    plans
ESOP planning/execution
Activity-based
    management
Open book management
Preparing the business
    for sale
Business valuation
Transition

Enhancements:
Reduce product/service
    cycle time
Expansion planning
Facilities investment
    planning
Resource allocation
Reviews
Equipment
Human resources
Facilities enhancement
Feasibility studies

Enhancements:
New product development
Back-end—ancillary
    product
Strategies

Enhancements:
Personal tax planning
Personal financial
    planning
Estate planning
Gift planning
Succession planning
Retirement planning
Wills, trusts, etc.
Portfolio management

- A highly structured organization and defined responsibilities.
- Compensation incentives based on meeting quantitative goals.[12]

Differentiation from Competitors

Differentiation from competitors, or *Product Innovation*, as a strategy requires management to create something that is perceived industry wide as being unique. This strategy allows premium pricing over the competition due to the brand loyalty of the customers. Generally, this strategy precludes the company from obtaining a high market share and is often associated with the concept of exclusivity. Products tend to be more costly due to the product design requirements, the additional research and development required, the high-quality materials used, or the level of customer service provided.

Uniqueness related to Product Innovation can be created via many approaches such as:

- Developing a design or brand image.
- Technology leadership.
- Product features provided.
- Level of or type of customer service provided.
- A strong dealer network.[13]

Highly successful product innovators generally differentiate themselves by using more than one approach. The differentiation strategy's commonly required skills and resources include:

- Possessing high-quality marketing skills.
- Strong product-engineering capabilities.
- A creative flair.
- A highly competent basic research team.
- A reputation for technological or quality leadership.
- Known tradition in the industry or a unique combination of skills drawn from related industries.
- A high level of cooperation from the channel of distribution.[14]

In addition, the strategy requires the development of many organizational characteristics including:

- Incentives based on subjective measures instead of definitive quantitative goals.

- A high level of cooperation and coordination between the research and development, product development, and marketing departments.
- Facilities and amenities capable of attracting scientist, engineers, creative individuals, or a highly skilled labor force.[15]

Focus on a Particular Buyer Group

Focus on a particular buyer group, segment of the product line or geographic area, or *Customer Intimacy*, as a strategy is based on being able to serve its highly focused target group more effectively or efficiently than its competitors. The competitors are assumed to be marketing to a more diverse market, geographic market, or with a broader product line.

Companies with this strategy have a low-cost position or a high degree of differentiation with its strategic target market or both. Differentiation for these companies will come from being better at meeting the needs of the target market or from a low-cost position related to the target market (although they may not be the low-cost provider for the industry as a whole).

A focus strategy for Customer Intimacy will require a combination of the same skills, resources, and organizational characteristics that are required for the Product Innovation strategy. Each of these strategies often need very different styles of leadership and usually evolve into their own unique corporate cultures. In addition, each of these strategies requires the use of different performance measures. Being a cost-efficient provider would necessitate a focus on performance measures related to manufacturing, while a strategy based on Product Innovation would focus on performance measures related to customer satisfaction and perceptions.

Strategy Risks

Understanding the appropriate use of each strategy requires having knowledge of the risks that are associated with each strategy. Risks related to a Cost Efficiencies strategy include:

- Technological advances making the prior capital investments obsolete.
- Lower-cost learning curve by newcomers to the industry and their ability to invest in state-of-the-art facilities without concern for write-offs of existing facilities and equipment.
- The extreme focus on cost, blinding management from spotting the need for product or marketing changes.
- Cost increases resulting from inflation eating away at strategy's cost advantages and not being able to offset the competitor's premium pricing due to their differentiation strategy.[16]

The risks associated with the strategy of Product Innovation include:

- The cost differential between the low-cost providers and the differentiated innovators becomes greater than the firm's ability to maintain its brand loyalty. Customers, at some point, are willing to sacrifice image, features, or service to benefit from large cost savings.
- Buyers' needs change, and they are no longer attracted to the company because of its differentiating characteristics.
- Imitation by competitors narrows or eliminates the perceived differentiation. This is especially true as industries mature and can be seen today in several industries, such as the software industry, furniture industry, automobile industry, and so forth.[17]

The strategy, based on a focus on a particular buyer group, segment of the product line, or geographic area through Customer Intimacy, has a different set of risks. These risks include:

- The cost advantages of serving an extremely focused target market become less than the cost savings of the low-cost provider serving a broad market.
- The differences in the products or services, desired by the target market and those desired by the marketplace, as a whole narrows or is eliminated.
- Competitors identify a submarket within the company's target market and effectively out-focus the company.[18]

Although all companies follow one of the three generic strategies, unless they find themselves "stuck in the middle," the strategies are developed uniquely by each company based on their marketplace and resources.

Company's Intangible Assets

Even if a company understands its strategy, it must gain an understanding of its intangible assets if it is to use them effectively. Companies often fail to capitalize on the opportunities offered by their intangible assets because they have never identified all the intangible assets they own. We have identified over 90 types of intellectual properties and intangible assets. An illustrative list has been included as Exhibit 1.3 in order to assist companies in the process of identifying their intellectual properties and intangible assets.

Intellectual capital is the value generator of the now and the future and should be an important consideration in each company's strategy plan. To sustain growth, companies have to:

Exhibit 1.3   *List of Intellectual Property*

These are identifiable and transferable, have a determinate life, and may not be subject to the day-to-day work efforts of the owner.

- Airport gates and slots
- Bank customers, including deposits, loans, trusts, and credit cards
- Blueprints
- Book libraries
- Brand names
- Broadcast licenses
- Buy-sell agreements
- Certificates of need
- Chemical formulas
- Computer software
- Computerized databases
- Contracts
- Cooperative agreements
- Copyrights
- Credit information files
- Customer contracts
- Customer and client lists
- Customer relationships
- Designs and drawings
- Development rights
- Distribution networks
- Distribution rights
- Drilling rights
- Easements
- Employment contracts
- Engineering drawings
- Environmental rights
- FCC licenses
- Favorable financing
- Favorable leases
- Film libraries
- Food flavorings and recipes

- Franchise agreements
- Historical documents
- HMO enrollment lists
- Insurance expirations
- Insurance in force
- Joint ventures
- Know-how
- Laboratory notebooks
- Landing rights
- Leasehold interests
- Literary works
- Loan portfolios
- Location value
- Management contracts
- Manual databases
- Manuscripts
- Medical charts and records
- Mineral rights
- Musical compositions
- Natural resources
- Newspaper morgue files
- Noncompete covenants
- Options, warrants, grants, rights
- Patent applications
- Patents (both product and process)
- Patterns
- Permits
- Prescription drug files
- Prizes and awards
- Procedural manuals
- Production backlogs
- Product designs

- Property use rights
- Proposals outstanding
- Proprietary computer software
- Proprietary processes
- Proprietary products
- Proprietary technology
- Publications
- Retail shelf space
- Royalty agreements
- Schematics and diagrams
- Securities portfolios
- Security interests
- Shareholder agreements
- Solicitation rights
- Stock and bond instruments
- Subscription lists
- Supplier contracts
- Technical and specialty libraries
- Technical documentation
- Technology sharing agreements
- Title plants
- Trade secrets
- Trained and assembled workforce
- Trademarks and trade names
- Training manuals
- Use rights (air, water, and land)

Source: Michael Mard and Joseph Agiato, Jr., *Consulting Services Practice Aid 99-2: Valuing Intellectual Property and Calculating Infringement Damages* (New York: AICPA, 1999), p. 1.15. Reprinted with permission.

- Identify the intellectual capital available to them.
- Measure the value of the intellectual capital components.
- Structure the means of delivery and potential leverage with other potential intellectual capital within the company.
- Manage the cash flow and the distribution channels of the intellectual capital.
- Protect the intellectual capital by converting it to intellectual property.
- Manage the intellectual property registrations on a worldwide basis.
- License intellectual property to and from third parties.
- Ensure compliance with all agreements.

Intellectual property is a subset of intangible assets—patents, copyrights, trademarks, and identifiable know-how. Again, we are simplifying by listing the major ones. Others are trade design, trade dress, and trade secrets.

Intangible assets are long-lived assets used in the production of goods and services that, unlike fixed or tangible assets, lack physical properties. Intangible assets represent certain long-lived legal rights or competitive advantages developed or acquired by a business enterprise. Intangible assets differ considerably in their characteristics and useful lives and are classified by the following characteristics:

- **Identifiably**—Patents, copyrights, franchises, trademarks, and other similar intangible assets that can be specifically identified with reasonably descriptive names.
- **Manner of acquisition**—Intangible assets that may be purchased or developed internally.
- **Determinate or indeterminate life**—Many intangible assets that have a determinate life established by law or by contract or economic behavior.
- **Transferability**—The right to a patent, copyright, or franchise that can be identified separately and bought or sold.

For strategic planning purposes, the intangible assets must be readily identifiable and capable of being separated from the other assets employed in the business. An intangible asset can be defined by referring to practical considerations such as whether it is supported by a contract, or by referring to whether it can be economically measured objectively with a determinate life. Intangible assets that exist but cannot be specifically identified are included in goodwill and not part of the planning process as they result from the overall strategic activities of the company.

For an identifiable intangible asset to exist from a valuation or economic perspective, it should possess certain attributes. These attributes are also necessary from a planning perspective. Some of the more common attributes include the following:

- It should be subject to specific identification and a recognizable description.
- It should be subject to the right of private ownership, and this private ownership must be legally transferable.
- There should be some tangible evidence or manifestation of the existence of the intangible asset (e.g., a contract, a license, a registration document, a computer diskette, a set of procedural documentation, a listing of customers, recorded on a set of financial statements, etc.).
- It should have been created or have come into existence at an identifiable time (or time period) or as the result of an identifiable event.
- It should be subject to being destroyed or to a termination of existence at an identifiable time (or time period) or as the result of an identifiable event.

In other words, there should be a specific bundle of rights (legal and otherwise) associated with the existence of any intangible asset.

To find out more about intangible and intellectual assets and reporting for them in financial statements see *Valuation for Financial Reporting: Intangible Assets, Goodwill, and Impairment Analysis, SFAS 141 and 142*, coauthored by Michael Mard, Jim Hitchner, and Steven D. Hyden, et. al., of the Financial Valuation Group.

For an identifiable intangible asset to have a quantifiable value from an economic analysis or appraisal perspective, it should possess certain additional attributes. These attributes are also necessary from a planning perspective. Some of the more common additional attributes include the following:

- The intangible asset should generate some measurable amount of economic benefit to its owner; this economic benefit could be in the form of an income increment or of a cost savings; this economic benefit is sometimes measured by comparison to the amount of income otherwise available to the intangible asset owner (e.g., the business) if the subject intangible asset did not exist.
- This economic benefit may be measured in a number of ways, such as net income, net operating income, or net cash flow.
- The intangible asset should be able to enhance the value of the other assets with which it is associated; the other assets may encompass all other assets of the business, including: tangible personal property, tangible real estate, or other intangible assets.

Some of the more common categories of intangible assets most commonly valued are as follows (see Exhibit 1.3 for a more detailed list):

- **Patents**—Product or process.
- **Brands**—Consumer goods' brands, trademarks, corporate names.
- **Publishing Rights**—Magazines, books, mastheads, film and music rights.
- **Intellectual Property**—Patents, copyrights, technology, know-how.
- **Licenses**—Television and radio, franchises, distribution rights.
- **Computer Software**—Developed in-house.

Intangible assets are often of little value independently but have significant value when used in bundles. The easiest example is a technology like the cell phone. The cell phone is based on a multitude of patents and will not work without all of them. Most of them have no value without the others. This is often referred to as a technical bundle of intangible assets. See Exhibit 1.4 for an illustrative list of the intangible assets typically included in marketing bundles, IT bundles, and technical bundles.

Economic phenomena that do not meet these specific attribute tests typically do not qualify as identifiable intangible assets. Some economic phenomena are merely descriptive in nature. They may describe conditions that contribute to the existence of—and value of—identifiable intangible assets. But these phenomena do not possess the requisite elements to distinguish themselves as intangible assets.

Exhibit 1.4	*Intangible Assets Included in Bundles*	
Marketing Bundle	**IT Bundle**	**Technical Bundle**
• Primary trademark	• Enterprise solutions	• Key patents
• Corporate name and logo	• Custom applications	• Trade secrets
• Marketing umbrella	• Data warehouses	• Formulae
• Sub-brand names	• Master licenses	• Packaging technology
• Core brand	• Source code	and sources
• Worldwide trademark	• Databases	• Shapes and sizes
registration	• Data mining	• Process technology
• Copyrights	• Domain names/URLs	• Design technology
• Secondary trademarks	• e-Commerce sites	• Proprietary test results
• Packaging design and	• Third-party software	• Plant and production
copyrights	tools	design
• Trade dress	• Credit/payment	• Product specifications
• Characters	systems	• Operating platforms

Source: © Copyright by Weston Anson, Consor Intellectual Asset Management. All rights reserved. Used with permission.

For a typical business, descriptive economic phenomena that do not qualify as identifiable intangible assets for accounting purposes may include:

- High market share
- High profitability
- General positive reputation
- Monopoly position
- Market potential

However, while these descriptive conditions do not qualify as identifiable intangible assets themselves, they may indicate the existence of identifiable intangible assets that do have substantial economic value. They are most often referred to collectively as goodwill.

Although these intangible assets do not meet the criteria for classification as identifiable and measurable intangible assets for financial-reporting purposes, they are often used as performance measures related to various performance areas.

Value Chains

Another method that can be used to analyze a company is the value chain. The value chain attempts to break the company into its many component parts (or performance areas) that are necessary for the company to operate. Typically the company is broken down into primary activities and supporting activities. With the value chain laid out, decisions can be made as to which corporate activities should be focused upon for improvement or are the key strategic activities of the company.

Many individuals and companies have developed value chain models. We have taken the models developed by Michael Porter and McKinsey & Company and combined them into one generic model. Supporting activities in our generic model include: infrastructure, technology, and human resources. Primary activities include: manufacturing, distribution, marketing, and service.

Exhibit 1.5 shows the generic value chain and its activity (performance area) descriptions. For example, under primary activities, manufacturing includes procurement activities and assembly activities. The supporting activities infrastructure area includes: planning, finance, management information systems, and legal services.

A value chain for a computer peripheral manufacturing company that designs, markets, and distributes its products, but outsources all the manufacturing activities, is presented in Exhibit 1.6. As can be seen, the various activities shown help one to understand the company and its complexity. From the value chain, you can

Exhibit 1.5   *The Generic Value Chain Developed by Combining the Porter and McKinsey Generic Value Chains*

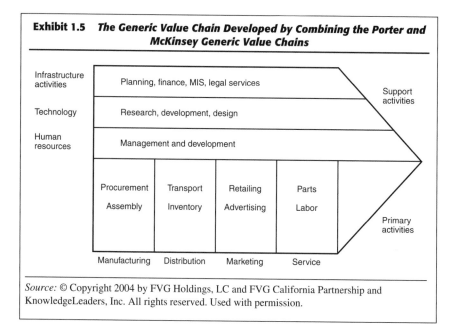

Source: © Copyright 2004 by FVG Holdings, LC and FVG California Partnership and KnowledgeLeaders, Inc. All rights reserved. Used with permission.

Exhibit 1.6   *Sample Computer Company Value Chain*

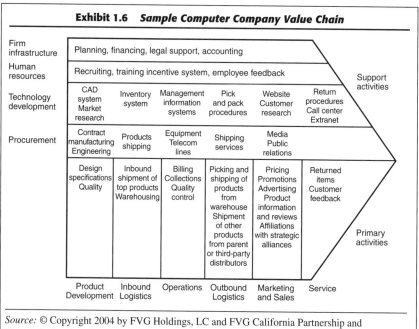

Source: © Copyright 2004 by FVG Holdings, LC and FVG California Partnership and KnowledgeLeaders, Inc. All rights reserved. Used with permission.

isolate the various performance areas of the company and focus discussions on each area and how it interacts with and helps or hurts related areas.

As the company refines its strategy and develops performance measures, the value chain will help define the performance areas that should be monitored as part of the performance measurement system, which in turn will help to increase the company's strategic effectiveness.

SWOT Analysis

One of the simplest but perhaps most effective methods for executives to use in analyzing their company is to perform a SWOT analysis of the company. SWOT analysis gets its name from the four concepts it attempts to analyze—the company's *s*trengths, *w*eaknesses, *o*pportunities, and *t*hreats. Using this simple framework will focus your activities into areas where you are strong and where the greatest opportunities lie, while requiring you to address your weaknesses and the new threats from your competitors or from technological advances.

There are many benefits to using a SWOT analysis in analyzing a company. The Malaspina University College website lists the following benefits and concerns about the use of SWOT analysis. Benefits include:

- A framework for identifying and analyzing strengths, weaknesses, opportunities, and threats.
- An impetus to analyze a situation and develop suitable strategies and tactics.
- A basis for assessing core capabilities and competences.
- The evidence for, and cultural key to, change.
- A stimulus to participation in a group experience.[19]

Hill and Westbrook argue that SWOT analysis is an overview approach that is unsuited to today's diverse and unstable markets.[20] They also suggest that it can be ineffective as a means of analysis because of:

- The generation of long lists.
- The use of description, rather than analysis.
- A failure to prioritize.[21]

It is interesting that the concerns listed are not really about the method itself but how individuals can misuse the analysis process or not complete a thorough analysis. Although we agree with the concerns in most companies, especially small ones, a consistent use of the SWOT analysis by management should lead to a more complete analysis of the company than the systems they are currently employing.

As can be seen in Exhibit 1.7, the SWOT analysis box also addresses internal and external forces. Strengths and weaknesses are both concerned with the internal analysis of the company, while the opportunities and threats are concerned with the external forces affecting the company.

As management develops its list of strengths, weaknesses, opportunities, and threats, they need to remember that for every positive attribute of the company there is a negative attribute. In contrast, every negative attribute has a positive attribute for the company. For example, if a company has the strength of having no competition it also has the threat of new competitors entering the marketplace. Another example relates to technology. If the competitors have established technology (your company's weakness) then the company has the opportunity to develop a better technological mousetrap.

Factors that can be considered when performing the SWOT analysis include:

- Quality and depth of management.
- Size of the company.
- Geographic and product line diversification.

Exhibit 1.7   SWOT Analysis

"SWOT" Analysis

Strengths (internal):	Weaknesses (internal):
• What do you do better than the competitors? • What intellectual property do you own?	• What do the competitors do better than you do? • What do you need to compete more effectively?
Opportunities (external):	**Threats (external):**
• What changes are occurring in the industry or in customer demands that you can take advantage of? • What weaknesses of your competitors can you take advantage of?	• What changes are occurring in the industry or in consumer demand that your competitors can take advantage of better than you can? • What are your competitors doing to attract your customers?

Source: © Copyright 2004 by FVG Holdings, LC and FVG California Partnership and KnowledgeLeaders, Inc. All rights reserved. Used with permission.

- Market position and penetration.
- Supplier and customer dependence.
- Product technology.
- Intellectual properties owned.
- Financial resources.
- Customer demographics.

When attempting to analyze each of these areas, management should ask itself questions similar to the ones below. As the executives brainstorm in each of the areas, they will expand the list to fit their circumstances and drill down to the level of detail needed to accomplish a complete analysis. Examples of questions for each area include:

- Strengths (the company's core competencies and resources):
  - What does the company do well?
  - How strong is the company in the market or what is its market position or share?
  - Does the company have a clear communicable vision or direction?
  - Does the company have a positive corporate culture that makes for a work environment that will attract the employees desired?
  - What are the company's definable resources (tangible and intangible)?
- Weaknesses (the company's liabilities in the competitive marketplace):
  - What systems could be improved at the company?
  - What does the company do poorly?
  - Does the company have the financial resources to purchase needed equipment, technology, or facilities?
  - Does the company have the financial resources to withstand a downturn or unforeseen negative circumstances?
  - Can the company support its growth rate?
- Opportunities (with the company's customers and in the marketplace):
  - What changes are taking place in the market that open up opportunities? Is the company positioned to take advantage of the opportunities?
  - Is the company entering new markets?
  - Can the company upgrade its technology to lower costs?
  - Can the company expand its geographic coverage?

- Can the company improve its use of the Internet for marketing or customer relations?
- Threats (what your competitors are doing and other potential challenges):
  - What obstacles do you face?
  - What are your competitors doing?
  - Are regulatory requirements or customer demands forcing a change in your products or services?
  - Is technology threatening your market position?
  - Is there pressure on your profit margins?

Using a SWOT analysis will allow management to articulate the strengths, weakness, opportunities and threats to the company. With this type of analysis, management can develop plans to create a better market position than its competitors and to gain market share.

Performance Areas, Performance Indicators, and Activity Measures

As can be seen from the Value Chain Analysis, every company has many performance areas. Performance areas are logical areas of focus based on how the business is organized and operates. Each business will divide the company into formal or informal performance areas, depending on the management style of the company and the practical resources available to them. As the business grows, the performance areas are divided because the corresponding growth in employees generally provides for a segregation of responsibilities and activities.

Performance areas typically include:

- Shipping
- Advertising and public relations
- Customer service
- Manufacturing
- Purchasing
- Research and development
- Warehousing
- Information technology (the computer department)

- Finance department
- Other

Each of the recognized performance areas can be monitored by performance indicators. Performance indicators are defined as measures that provide feedback to a team or managers about how the employee, team, or company is performing in reference to the established standards for performance in a particular performance area.

The established standards are referred to as benchmarks. In order for benchmarks to be meaningful, they should have certain characteristics:

- Point of reference from which measurements can be made.
- Serves as a standard against which performance can be measured or judged.
- Can be internally or externally based.
- Must be consistent—not subject to external factors causing variations.
- Reasonably achievable given the company's allocation and apportionment of resources.
- Capable of being maintained over a long period of time (not a sprint, but a marathon).

Examples of performance measures tied to performance areas are:

Performance Area	Example Performance Indicator
Customer Service	Number of customer contacts
Manufacturing	Amount of rework
Human Resources	Employee turnover

Drilling down into the performance area, we find each performance indicator is affected by one or more activity measures. Activity measures are defined as specific procedures or processes in a performance area. These measures are input items for a specific performance indicator and must be able to be consistently measured. To be an effective measure the activity must be definable, documented, and have a performance standard established. One of the greatest problems for small businesses is the lack of internal systems to capture the data necessary to measure an activity and to compare it to a set performance standard. The performance indicator Employee turnover is controlled primarily by employee satisfaction. Employee's satisfaction is affected by activity measures like the percentage of employee suggestions acted upon or the amount of training they are receiving to improve their skill levels.

Examples of performance indicators and related activity measures can be seen in the following table:

Performance Indicator	*Related Activity Measure*
Number of customer contacts	Actual number of calls initiated
	Actual number of connections made
Amount of rework	Percentage of raw materials inspected
	Error rate per shift
Employee turnover	Tardiness and absentee rate
	Employee suggestions acted on

When analyzing a company's performance measures, management must look at the performance measures from a variety of perspectives. Newton's law states that for every action there is an equal and opposite reaction. The law of performance measurement is that for every perspective there is an equally important and opposite perspective. The key to success lies in balancing the perspectives, seeing the business from several views. Management must look at every measure from the various viewpoints such as:

Short-term versus long-term—During hard economic times a company might be tempted to focus on short-term profitability and cash flow–producing measures. In the early 1990s many companies felt the sting of that perspective when they cut their marketing and sales efforts and, as a result, lost significant market share. The tradeoff of a short- versus long-term perspective ended up costing many companies significantly more to regain lost market share than the short-term savings they realized.

Internal versus external (customer)—A tradeoff between an internal and an external, customer-focused perspective was created with the advent of voice-mail technology. There is no question that implementing a voice-mail system made sense from a cost standpoint. However, many companies received negative feedback from customers because of that choice. Companies, in the habit of measuring and responding to customer feedback, quickly made adjustments to their system; continually tweaking the system to find the right balance between company and customer needs. Those companies who were simply focused on cost savings did not feel the negative impact of that choice until it was too late.

Global versus local—In addition to measuring progress toward a company's "big-picture" plan, a large company, such as Wal-Mart, must also pay attention to how its image plays out in the local communities that its workforce and customers come from. For example, Wal-Mart has been known to pull a controversial item from its stores to appease public opinion. Much of Wal-Mart's success stems from maintaining the ideal balance between being a huge, global conglomerate and the local, friendly next-door neighbor.

Inputs versus outputs—Using a nonbusiness example—In the past, many nonprofits and government agencies were evaluated on how they managed their funds. Today, they are held to a higher standard; they must also measure and report on the impact that those funds had on their constituents. We see this standard really taking hold in public schools. More and more, schools are funded and teachers compensated, not just on how many hours they work or students they teach but on the actual success rates of their pupils.

Like schools, foundations and philanthropists who have always demanded accountability about the use of contributed funds have raised the bar and now expect some measurable, tangible evidence of successful outcomes. In the case of nonprofits, having a performance measurement system in place helps to maintain the charter the entity was created under and prevents a random change of direction that often happens with an ever-rotating board of directors, each with his or her own agenda.

Lagging versus leading—Leading indicators are financial and nonfinancial indicators that imply some affect on the company in the future. For example, if customer complaints are on the rise, this most likely implies that if the company does not fix the cause of the complaints customers will look for and move to another supplier of the product or service. Lagging indicators are indicators that show how we have performed in the past but offer no direct insight into performance in the future. Bankers are especially sensitive to the need for a balanced perspective in this area. They know that past performance is no promise of future outcomes. As a result, banks often require, in their loan covenants, that a company submit a regular flash report that includes leading indicators such as: work in progress, backlog, standing orders, returns and refunds, customer complaints, defective shipments, and so forth.

Value-added versus non-value-added—In an attempt to minimize waste, many organizations are making distinctions about activities that add value to the company versus those that do not. For example, investing in new equipment may add value; investing in new equipment due to lack of proper maintenance does not.

Soft versus hard—Just as we need hard measures like a productivity percentage, we also need a corresponding soft measure like employee morale to monitor the effects of an increased demand on productivity. Soft measures can be harder to quantify, but in the overall scheme of things can be even more meaningful than hard measures. For example, customer attrition is a hard, very quantifiable measure. Customer satisfaction is considered a soft measure; however, with the right measurement system it is easy to determine some of the leading causes of dissatisfaction (i.e., late delivery, product quality, damage on arrival, etc.) that ultimately lead to customer attrition. A good balance of both soft and hard measures provides deeper insights into the ramifications of company policy.

Financial versus nonfinancial—This distinction is so basic to performance measurement that it seems silly to even mention it here. However, as basic as it is, it is surprising how many companies rely solely on financial measurements.

Here are some examples of nonfinancial measures and how important they can be to company success:

Quality of output as a balance to quantity of output—It is possible to have a high mark in quantity of output and be lulled into a false sense of security. Only when quantity is measured against quality are the numbers valid.

Customer satisfaction within a context of issue relevance—For example: a company may score high in an area that has very little relevance to customer needs. For instance, the color of the packaging may seem important and may even get good reviews from customers, but within the overall context of a hierarchy of needs, the customer may put more weight on other factors that ultimately have a greater impact on the relationship. The weighting of measures plays a critical role in the performance measurement process.

Total costs associated with employee turnover—Including hiring costs, lost productivity, reduction of quality, team morale, and so forth. For companies dealing with a highly competitive hiring environment, this information will have a huge impact on compensation planning. Companies who understand this have found creative ways to channel monies previously spent on employee turnover issues into far more productive rewards for employees, while at the same time, serving the overall goals of the company.

Employee training—Not just dollars spent, but overall effectiveness of training. Coincidentally, there is a direct correlation between training effectiveness, productivity, and team morale. Team morale has a significant effect on customer satisfaction. By studying the dominoes-like structure of activities in an organization, it is easy to see how important nonfinancial measures can be when it comes to predicting future outcomes.

R&D productivity—Average development cycle times, attempts versus failures, average investment per new product, marketplace acceptance, and so forth. Monitoring these numbers has lead many companies to "buy" rather than develop new technology given the true cost of development.

Nonfinancial performance measures can often be extremely important in managing various aspects of the company. Let us use a large transportation company for the handicapped as an example. The company has 200 vans and limos adapted for the handicapped. A key nonfinancial measurement for this company would be "miles per gallon per vehicle per driver." The measurement would be a leading indicator for several items:

- **Maintenance needed on the vehicle**—Low miles per gallon is often a good indicator of poor engine performance (a performance issue), implying that vehicle maintenance may be required.
- **Increased risks**—In addition, it could also be a people issue. The company found that a driver with lower mileage in the same vehicle than other drivers generally had poor driving habits. There was a high probability that the driver was a "fast-and-slow," "start-and-stop" type of driver who increased the company's risk related to:
  - Accidents
  - Tickets
  - Client complaints

The owner of the company discovered his insurance premiums were increasing significantly and that by improving the driving habits of the drivers or replacing drivers he could reduce insurance costs, accident repairs, and more importantly customer complaints. An added bonus was that he could use part of the cost reductions to establish a bonus pool to reward the good drivers who met or exceeded the performance standards.

The key to all these various perspective distinctions is to make sure that the measures you select for your company provide a balanced view. As we said earlier, performance measures tell us if we are on track to achieve our goals. They also tell us if our goals are the right goals to have. What may have seemed like a worthy goal on the surface may in fact create a multitude of other problems. In others words, the cure can be worse than the cold. The term "growing broke" describes a common scenario in smaller businesses that are losing money. The company sets a goal to increase sales, but without properly analyzing the source of the losses, the company can end up compounding previous losses.

From the many performance indicators possible within every company, management must determine the key performance indicators for their company. These key indicators are related to the company's critical success factors, which are discussed later in the chapter.

What Is a Performance Measurement System?

A performance measurement system is a mechanism for capturing and reporting performance indicators. The system is most effective when implemented on a real-time basis. Performance measurement systems vary from a low-tech columnar pad or electronic spreadsheet to very high-tech computerized systems with dashboards and fancy graphing capabilities. The value is not in the low- or high-tech systems used, but in picking the right performance indicators to monitor and improve performance.

There are two primary benefits of a performance measurement system:

1. To improve the availability and quality of information for decision makers, and
2. To stimulate desired behavior by providing performance feedback (preferably in real time) on activities that are most critical to company success.

The model in Exhibit 1.8 provides a big picture view of the system. A performance measurement system has four evolutionary stages. In the first stage, people and processes are generating data to be collected. The data is fed into and organized by various information systems such as a general ledger, point-of-sale system, manufacturing resource planning (MRP) system, customer relationship management (CRM) system, time and billing system, and so on. Once the information is organized, it is interpreted using various analyses and modeling tools. At this stage, we are looking to glean specific knowledge about how the people and systems are performing. Finally, that knowledge is paired with new strategies for improvement, which are then applied to the business. Many companies stop there, only using the information to influence the decision-making process. Although there is value in that, the real value of a performance measurement system lies in providing real-time feedback to those involved in the activities that generated the data in the first place.

Here is an interesting angle on this whole approach: Often the very act of providing feedback stimulates better performance without management's input. Does this mean that the employees themselves can apply their own wisdom to the work environment? Absolutely! In fact, one of the greatest benefits of a performance measurement system is how employees respond to feedback by taking ownership of their actions rather than always waiting to be led by management.

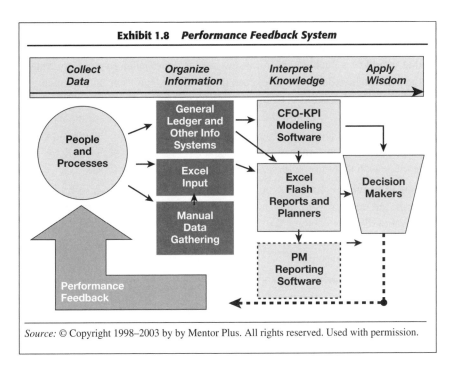

Exhibit 1.8 *Performance Feedback System*

Successful Performance Measurement Systems

Successful performance measurement systems have common characteristics. These characteristics serve as a checklist in designing and implementing a performance measurement system.

- **Linked to primary goals and strategies**—The measurement process can become burdensome and irrelevant if we measure everything. When you measure everything, nothing is important. Goals and strategies serve as a filter to cull out the most meaningful measures.

- **Clearly defined**—One of the most common reasons for poor performance is poorly articulated expectations. Performance expectations must be made explicit. Employees must fully embrace the expectations to buy into and support a measurement process. This tenet often leads to the development and documentation of policies and procedures. Often, this activity alone improves performance once employees understand what is expected of them.

- **Understandable**—The language used to describe a particular measure must survive the authors of the measurement system. Any terminology that does not transcend all levels of personnel is subject to suspicion and feigned ignorance. "How can I be held accountable to something I don't understand?"

- **Easily measured**—In some cases the costs associated with monitoring a particular measure may outweigh the benefits. Although there may be a number that would be valuable to monitor, the cost of developing a system to capture the performance data may far exceed the potential savings or improvement associated with that activity. Companies make tradeoffs like this everyday. In his book *Extraordinary Guarantees*,[22] Christopher Hart cites the example of how credit card companies have found that the cost of reviewing the credit performance of every customer is far more expensive than the cost of bad debt. This is the reason that our mailboxes are full of instant credit options.

- **Few in number**—Keep it simple. Although there may be dozens of measures across an entire organization, when it comes to flash reports and short-term scoreboards, less is more. We want to avoid a situation where the act of supporting the performance measurement system takes preeminence over the activities being measured.

- **Reported regularly**—How soon they forget. It is a bit of a cliché but very true in performance measurement. Once you begin the feedback process, employees will come to expect a regular report. Irregularities in reporting frequency may cause people to question how important and committed the company is to a performance measurement program.

- **Consistent follow-through**—An owner of a small lighting store began posting her average sale on a daily basis. Within days, the average sale began to rise. Within a month, the average sale went from $63 to $84 dollars. She continued this for a few months and then went on vacation. While she was away, the average sale was not being monitored. When she returned three weeks later her average sale had dropped dramatically. Moral of the story: employees will care about the measures only as much as you do. Only a persistent focus will produce lasting results. To finish the story, she began to monitor and post her average sale again and within a week, it came close to the benchmark previously established.

- **Openly shared**—In the past, performance information was a closely held secret among managers. To have an effective performance measurement process employees need to have access to the information. To avoid suspicion managers should avoid "massaging" and selectively sharing the data. Employees want the whole truth and nothing but the truth. Once again, if we want them to act like owners, we have to treat them accordingly.

- **Predictive in nature**—The right set of measurements should serve as an indicator of future outcomes. For example, the owner of an insurance brokerage company noticed an increase in call volume. Her receptionist was swamped. She took that as a sign that her new advertising campaign was working, and she should continue that expenditure. However, before making that decision, she dug deeper and found that although the advertising was generating more calls, the prospects were not as qualified as in previous campaigns. As it turned out, call volume was not as good a predictor as it had been in the past. She modified the prospect intake process to include a question regarding prospects' current insurance policy. Positive responses to this single question turned out to be a more reliable predictive indicator of future sales.

- **Developed by everyone**—It is all about buy-in. The more you can involve the team in the development of measures that relate to their role in the company the more likely they will be to support and trust the process. Many companies have made the mistake of "handing down" a prescribed set of measures and expecting the team to accept them. When we can step back and trust the process, more often than not, the team will devise the same set of measures as the managers would, but because they coauthored the measures, there is a greater commitment to the measurement system and their personal performance.

- **Team or unit based**—Measuring performance on an individual level is important, but if it is the only type of measure used it tends to create a "me first" culture. Whereas when we measure behavior on a collective basis we are much more likely to see team-oriented behavior.

- **Tested against behavioral outcomes**—A furniture manufacturer ran into problems when he put so much emphasis on getting product "out the door" that there was a significant increase in defective product back "in the door." In this case, a productivity measure was out of balance without a corresponding quality measure.

- **Assessed and modified regularly**—A wise man once said, "The only constant in life *and business* is change." The goals and strategies of a company will change over time. Performance measures will shift to reflect those changes. Performance measures help us overcome weaknesses and exploit opportunities. As we improve in a given area the emphasis of measurement will transfer to other areas.

- **Linked to compensation**—This is where the "rubber meets the road" in a performance measurement system. As the saying goes, "That which gets measured gets done. That which gets *rewarded* gets done again." Linking compensation to performance can yield the traction needed to really get the program up and running.

Benefits of Scorecard Performance Measurement System

According to the study on scorecard performance measurement systems sponsored by the American Institute of Certified Public Accountants (AICPA) the biggest benefit to the companies implementing performance measurement systems is "communicating strategy throughout the organization and alignment of employee behavior with organizational goals."[23]

There is a close relationship between the comprehensiveness of the performance measurement system and the benefits achieved. The more the system utilizes performance all the way down to the individual level, the greater the benefits realized by the company. If the performance measurements are linked to compensation and rewards then even greater benefits will be realized.

Companies that get the most benefit from the scorecard type performance systems generally have the following key characteristics:

- Have developed the performance system to focus on the key points of the company's corporate strategy.
- Have a comprehensive system focused on the company as a whole and not a particular area of the company.
- Have compensation and reward systems that are tied to the individual and group performance.
- Are accepted by and used by the employees.

The most important of these characteristics is the linkage of the performance system to the corporate strategy of the company.

Critical Success Factors

Every business has critical success factors that will increase revenue, reduce costs, or increase efficiencies. Management can define or discover the critical success factors of the company for every performance area in the company.

In our readings, we found a definition of critical success factors (CSFs) that we believe will provide insight for those trying to understand CSFs:

> Critical success factors are the limited number of areas in which satisfactory results will ensure successful competitive performance for the individual, department, or organization. Critical success factors are the few key areas where "things must go right" for the business to flourish and for the manager's goals to be attained.[24]

To add some illustrative examples of CSFs, Dr. Sheila Kessler (*www.competitiveedge.com*) has developed a list of CFSs for customers in a variety of industries. See Exhibit 1.9 for the CSFs for 16 different industries.

The airline industry is one that all of us can associate with, because most of us fly occasionally or frequently. The customers of the airline industry, based on Dr. Kessler's research, find the following factors (CSFs) important to their choice of an airline and the continued use of that airline:

- Baggage system
- Reservation system
- On-time arrivals
- Friendly service
- Good problem solving
- Competitive pricing
- Available flights
- Frequent flyer program
- Quality of meals
- Safety[25]

All of us would agree that if an airline provided us with all of the above 10 factors we would use that airline.

Identifying "those things that must go right" is one of the primary responsibilities of management. Depending on the strategy the company has chosen, the CSFs will vary even within the same market. Based on our experience, we believe that CSFs have the following characteristics that management can consider when developing their own:

- Has a material impact on the bottom line and strategic effectiveness.
- Directly affects successful competitive performance of company.
- Usually less than 10 factors in any one company.[26]
- Most likely affects customer satisfaction, directly or indirectly.
- Must be related to the company's strategy.

We agree that there are probably less than 10 critical success factors for any business. This is especially true of the small company. Even if there were more than 10 CSFs in small to midsized businesses (SMBs), these companies would not have the management depth to focus on more than a few CSFs at any one time. Management of SMBs may need to occasionally change their primary focus of the performance measurement system, which would allow a rotating emphasis year by year between major themes.

Exhibit 1.9 Critical Success Factors to Customers

Based on over 200 wallet-share projects. Note segments may vary within each industry.

Auto manufactures (low end)
Reliability and reputation
Safety
Appearance
Roominess and comfort
Feel of driving
Features
Price
Availability
Depreciation
Insurance costs
Warranty

Customized manufacturing
Good needs assessment
Good design/prototype review
On-time delivery
Reliability of product
Ease-of-use
Problem solving
Warranty policy
Invoice accuracy and ease

Restaurants
Clean
Competitively priced
Accurate service
Timely service
Friendly service
Menu selection
Facility (light, table, size)
Ambiance (décor)
Location
Food presentation
Theme

Distribution
Availability
Just-in-time delivery
Accuracy of order
Damage free delivery
Change communication
Special order handling
Competitive pricing
Real-time monitoring
Invoice accuracy and ease
Appearance
Helpful delivery
Good EDI system

Engineering and Construction
Reputation and financial stability
Close-out process
Delivers on time
Consistency of delivery
Real time monitoring
Good change order process
Competitively priced (units)
Rework percent
Report accuracy and timing
Best practice communication
Electronic compatibility

Hotels (business traveler)
Location
Competitive pricing
Room size
Comfort-bed, lighting, a/c
Cleanliness
Consistency (for chain)
Speed of check-in/out
Friendly service
Accuracy of systems
Maintenance
Ambiance
Good reservation system

Airlines
Baggage system
Reservation system
On-time arrivals
Friendly service
Good problem solving
Competitively priced
Available flights
Frequent flyer program
Quality of meals
Safety

Banks (for businesses)
Fees
Privacy
Ease of loans and flexibility
Location

Banks (for individuals)
Competitive fees and rates
Accuracy
Friendly, helpful staff
Location
Little or no waiting
ATM/electronic adequacy

Computers (business)
Competitively priced/features
Speed and storage
Executive training
Reliability
Technical support ease
Ease-of-changes to system
Warranty
Salability

Cellular
Quality of coverage
Price
Reliability
Promotions
Invoicing (no surprises)
Ease-of-use
Size of unit

VCRs
Ease of installation
Ease of use
Competitively priced
Return policies
Reliability
Reputation
Warranty policy
Product training

Electricity (business)
Predictable invoice
Dedicated service rep
Consistency of power
Least # of outages
Outage recovery
Good problem solving
Competitive pricing
Consultative sales

Car insurance
Price
Claim handling
Word-of-mouth
Coverage exclusions
Agency service
Top-of-mind
Sales ease

Pulp and paper chemicals
Assurance and availability
Consultative sales
Competitive pricing
Location
On-site service
Consistency of product
Quality of product

Groceries (67% impulse)
Safety
Availability
Taste
Competitive pricing
Appeal (ads and packaging)
Promotions (coupons, sales)
Ease-of-purchase (check-out)
Nutrition
Specific hunger or thirst

Medical supplies (business)
Safety and reliability
Productivity enhancement
Ease-of-ordering/invoicing
Competitive pricing
Availability
Product training

Key Performance Indicators

Every critical success factor has various performance indicators that affect it. Since management can only manage a limited number of items, it is important to select the most important performance indicators for that CSF, and these are called key performance indicators (KPIs).

KPIs have unique characteristics that management must consider when selecting them:

- Relate to a specific procedure or process.
- Are an input item for a specific performance indicator.
- Must have consistency of measurement.
- Must be able to be impacted by persons responsible for them.

The art of selecting KPIs requires that management understand how the CSFs and their KPIs are significant components of the company's corporate strategy. If the KPIs or benchmarks do not support the strategy, management will not be as effective as possible in advancing the company's market position, ROE, or cash flow and its resulting value.

Conclusion

To be able to competently assess the company's current state, management must complete a qualitative and quantitative analysis of the company. The full implications of the quantitative analysis cannot be derived from the numbers without an understanding of the company's qualitative factors.

Qualitative analysis of the company's current state requires that management:

- Use an analysis framework such as Porter's Five Forces or McKinsey's 7-S to analyze the industry and macroenvironmental influences.
- Articulate the company's corporate strategy and the related skills and resources required to carry out the strategy and define the risks associated with the particular strategy chosen.
- Develop a complete list of all the company's intangible assets and intellectual properties that can be used to advance the company's corporate strategy.
- Perform a SWOT analysis highlighting the company's strengths, weaknesses, opportunities, and threats.
- List the company's current critical success factors and the related key performance indicators. Benchmarks currently utilized for the KPIs should be documented.

- Assess the company's ability to capture the data required to compute and analyze the KPIs.

As management moves through the SBfV Process, managers will discover that it is designed to assist in assessing the company's current state and to begin the long-term process of moving from the current state to the desired future state. The advantage of the SBfV Model is that it takes the company on a gradual process of advancement instead of attempting to implement a comprehensive, costly system immediately.

QUANTITATIVE ANALYSIS OF THE COMPANY'S CURRENT STATE

A review of the company's current state would not be complete without a review of the company's performance measures. The level of review depends on the quality and depth of the management information systems employed within the company. In some companies, a wealth of information is available and in other companies, much of the information, especially for the nonfinancial performance measures, will need to be developed over time.

Performance Measures

Performance measures should be considered in terms of the analytical information they provide. Each of the performance measures provides management with information about one or more of the company's resources or capabilities, which are often thought of as the attributes of the company.

In order to understand the company and the operating and strategy implications of the performance measures (the key value of the analytical process), the company's resources need to be organized into a consistent framework. A company's resources are often grouped into four categories, which have been described by Jay Barney as:

Financial capital—All the different money resources that firms can use to conceive and implement strategies—capital from entrepreneurs, equity holders, bondholders, and banks' financial capital. Retained earnings are also an important type of financial capital.

Physical capital—The physical technology used in a firm, a firm's plant and equipment, its geographic location, and its access to raw materials. Specific examples of physical capital are a firm's computer hardware and software technology, robots used in manufacturing, and automated warehouses used to control inventory costs. Geographic location, as a type of physical capital, is an important resource.

Human capital—The training, experience, judgment, intelligence, relationships, and insight of individual managers and workers in a firm.

Organizational capital—An attribute of collections of individuals. Organizational capital includes a firm's formal reporting structure (what Penrose called the administrative framework); its formal and informal planning, controlling, and coordinating systems; and its culture and reputation; as well as informal relations among groups within a firm and between a firm and those in its environment.[27]

We believe, for management purposes, that the company's resources should be consistently grouped into six categories. While the additional categories of customer capital and systems capital could easily be folded into Barney's four categories, we believe that adding two categories would increase management's emphasis on these categories.

Therefore, the SBfV Model views the company's performance measures to be related to its:

- Financial capital
- Physical capital
- Human capital
- Organizational capital
- Customer capital
- Systems capital

The company's performance measures must be analyzed in order to monitor its ongoing progress from year to year, to compare its performance to industry comparative benchmarks and to be used in the strategic planning process.

Comparisons of the company's performance from year to year allow management to identify areas where the company has improved and areas of decline that may cause serious problems in the near term or over time. Comparison to industry ratios allows management to identify areas that give the company a competitive advantage or areas that can be improved when competitors have demonstrated where superior results can be achieved. Investors look at a company's internal improvements and analytical results that are superior to those achieved by competitors as being value-enhancing characteristics of a company.

Performance measures are generally based on data from:

- The company's financial and operational data.
- Industry financial and operational data.
- Surveys related to:
  - Customers
  - Suppliers
  - Lenders
  - Competitors
  - Stockholders
  - Employees

From this data it is possible to develop more ratios than can be managed or that will provide useful insight into the company. It has been estimated that there are over 3,000 potential performance measures. Individuals responsible for managing particular areas of performance normally cannot manage more than 6 to 8 performance measures. Many consultants recommend that the maximum number of managed performance measures be four.

Management must use care to develop meaningful ratios that will be used as the basis for management decisions without burying themselves in excess details. The higher the level of management the more summary analysis should be utilized. Management can ask lower levels of management for additional details and insight into the causes of the identified changes or deficiencies.

SBfV provides a systematic approach to analyzing the company's performance measures, which will provide insight into the company's usage of its resources and monitor whether the company is creating value for the stockholders.

Company Resources

Company resources are monitored by specific performance measures or by multiple performance measures. It should be noted that many performance measures (specifically when combined with others) could be used to monitor more than one of the company's resources.

Each industry and company may have competitive resources that are different than those of other industries or companies. This section is not a comprehensive presentation of all available performance measures but rather provides examples of some of the more common performance measures used in many, if not most, industries.

Financial capital—This is related to a company's capital structure and its use of funds from investors and vendors. Resources related to a company's financial capital include, the company's:

- Borrowing capacity
- Ability to raise capital
- Retention of prior earnings
- Sustainable growth rate

Human capital—Is related to the company's employees, the assets that walk out the door each night or at the end of each shift. These measures focus on the employees' capabilities to perform their responsibilities and to work together as a coordinated team. Resources related to a company's human capital include the employees':

- Education
- Training
- Knowledge
- Commitment
- Leadership ability
- Trust
- Integrity
- Experience

Physical capital—This is related to all the tangible resources owned or leased by the company. These measures are focused on the company's utilization and management of the tangible assets. Resources related to the company's physical capital include the company's:

- Productive capacity
- Capital expenditures
- Maintenance quality
- Flexibility and mixed use of fixed assets
- Technological commitment
- Location, location, location (access to suppliers, customers, and human capital)

Organizational capital—This is related to the company's group attributes, such as its culture, creativity, public image, and organizational structure. Resources related to the company's organizational capital include its:

- Employee loyalty
- Employee teamwork
- Reputation

- Product innovation
- Speed and quality of decision making

Customer capital—This is related to the company's relationship to its customers and the acceptance of its products by its customers and potential customers. Resources related to the company's customer capital include:

- Customer services
- Customer loyalty
- Market penetration
- Information access

Systems capital—This is related to the effectiveness of the company's identifiable operating systems. Resources related to the company's system capital include the company's:

- Computer systems and information systems
- Customer relationship management systems
- Communication systems
- Shop floor systems
- Inventory control systems
- Sales and marketing systems
- Accounting systems
- Project management systems

A company's ability to gather timely and sufficient decision-making information internally and externally exists today because of the advances made in the use of technology within the modern business. The only limitation is management's own failure to expand the company's data collection and analysis systems to fit the needs of the company's management team.

One caution: with the proliferation of PCs with independent spreadsheets and databases, all resources must be synchronized and verified to be useful in performance measurement.

Internally generated information can be captured in many instances in real time. For external information, prior to the Internet, an individual might have to wait for the hard copy version of the results of certain survey information with which to make his subject company comparisons. During the 1990s, the Internet dramatically enhanced our ability to obtain and disseminate information dramatically. Information that was once privately owned or perhaps available only to experts is now widely accessible, almost instantaneously. The availability and accessibility of all of this data provides the analyst with an expanded tool set to utilize to achieve deeper insights into the strengths, weaknesses, opportunities, and threats of a given company or industry.

Financial Statement Data

The most recognized and commonly used performance measures are based on the company's financial statements. Financial statements are the summaries of the recorded historical events and transactions of the company. In order to have financial statements that can be compared with similar companies within the industry, the financial statements may need to be modified for economic or normalizing adjustments in terms of their format.

One of the objectives of financial statement analysis is to ensure that the historical financial statements that can provide the basis for any forward-looking estimates or decision making reliably reflect the true operating performance of the enterprise. Therefore, the historical accounting financial statements may need to be adjusted (modified) for certain items that in the management's judgment, distort the true economic operating performance of the business.

Financial statement adjustments are made for a variety of reasons including:

- To develop historical earnings from which to predict future earnings.
- To present historical financial information on a normalized basis, that is, under normal operating conditions.
- To adjust for accounting practices that are a departure from industry or GAAP (Generally Accepted Accounting Principles) standards.
- To facilitate a comparison of a given company to itself, to other companies within the same industry, or to an accepted industry standard.
- To compare the debt and capital structure of the company to that of its competition or peers.
- To compare compensation with industry norms.

An adjustment to historical financial statements should be made if the effect of the adjustment will more accurately present the true operating performance of the enterprise. Therefore, all appropriate adjustments should be made, regardless of whether they reflect positively or negatively on the company. It is important to disclose the key assumptions underlying all adjustments.

To facilitate proper analysis and interpretation of a company's financial statements, these accounting statements should first be adjusted to reflect the economic realities of "normal" operating conditions. The objective of normalizing historical financial statements is to present the data on a basis comparable to that of other companies in the industry, thereby allowing benchmarking of the strength or weakness of the subject company relative to its peers.

Normalization generally involves adjusting for a number of broad categories:

- Unusual items
- Nonrecurring items
- Extraordinary items
- Nonoperating items
- Changes in accounting principles
- Nonconformance with GAAP
- Degree of ownership interest, including whether the interest has control

Unusual items are events or transactions that possess a high degree of abnormality and are of a type clearly unrelated to, or only incidentally related to, the ordinary and typical activities of the entity, taking into account the environment in which the entity operates.

Nonrecurring items are events or transactions that are not reasonably expected to recur in the foreseeable future, taking into account the environment in which the entity operates.

Extraordinary items are events or transactions that are distinguished by their unusual nature and by the infrequency of their occurrence. Thus, for an item to be classified as extraordinary, the item must be *both* an unusual item and a nonrecurring item.

Revenues or expenses that are unusual, nonrecurring, or extraordinary usually are removed from the historical data because they can distort the picture of the ongoing earning power of the business. Caution is advised, however, in that items that might be deemed unusual and infrequent in one industry might not be deemed so in another.

Items representative of the type of adjustments made to historical financial statements for unusual, nonrecurring, and extraordinary items include:

- Strikes and other types of work stoppages (unless common for the industry).
- Litigation expenses or recoveries.
- Uninsured losses due to unforeseen disasters such as fire or flood.
- One-time realization of revenues or expenses due to nonrecurring contracts.
- Gain or loss on the sale of a business unit or business assets.
- Discontinuation of operations.
- Insurance proceeds received on the life of a key person or from a property or casualty claim.

To achieve a clear picture of true operating performance for benchmarking purposes, the analyst may wish to remove nonoperating assets and liabilities and their related earnings or expenses from the subject's historical financial statements. Common examples of nonoperating items include:

- Excess cash.

- Marketable securities (if in excess of reasonable needs of the business).

- Real estate (if not used in business operations, or, in some situations, if the business could operate in rented facilities).

- Private planes, entertainment, or sports facilities (hunting lodge, transferable season ticket contracts, skyboxes, etc.).

- Antiques, private collections, and so forth.

Management must understand the effect that a change in accounting principles has on a company's financial statements. Some common examples of changes in accounting principles are:

- A change in the method of pricing inventory, such as LIFO (last in, first out) to FIFO (first in, first out) or FIFO to LIFO.

- A change in the method of depreciating previously recorded assets, such as from straight-line method to accelerated method or from accelerated method to straight-line method.

- A change in the method of accounting for long-term construction-type contracts.

- A change in or from the full-cost method of accounting in the extractive industries.

Such changes in accounting principles can result in irregular or inconsistent historic results. In essence, the yardstick becomes expandable or shrinks. For benchmarking purposes, management must do the best job possible in maintaining consistency between the accounting principles used by the companies in the benchmarking data and the accounting principles used by the subject company.

Public companies tend to choose accounting treatments that please shareholders by making earnings appear higher. Most closely held businesses' owners tend to elect an accounting treatment that minimizes earnings, thus minimizing the corporate tax burden. These choices may mean that if the financial statements of a private company have not been audited or reviewed, the accounting practices adopted by management may not comply with GAAP. The analyst may choose to make adjustments to bring them into or closer to GAAP compliance so that the subject's financial results can be compared to the financial results of its publicly held industry counterparts, if available and applicable. Adjustments may also be made to calculate cash flow. Examples of commonly encountered areas of non-conformance with GAAP are:

- Financial statements prepared on a tax or cash accounting basis.
- Unrecorded revenue in cash businesses.
- Inadequate bad debt reserve (or use of specific write-off method).
- Understated amounts of inventory, failure to write off obsolete or slow-moving inventory, and other inventory accounting issues.
- Unrecorded liabilities such as capital lease obligations, workforce-related costs (wages, sick, and vacation pay, etc.), deferred income taxes.
- Capitalization expense policies for fixed assets and prepaid expenses.
- Fixed asset write-off policies.
- Depreciation methods.
- Accounting for investments in subsidiaries or affiliated entities.
- Timing of revenue expense recognition for contract accounting, installment sales, warranties, subscriptions, and the like.

Finally, adjustments are made to eliminate self-serving biases of a controlling shareholder and put the company on an even keel with the benchmarked companies. Examples of such commonly encountered adjustments are:

- Smoothing of excess or deficient compensation or perquisites.
- Elimination of discretionary expenses and operating inefficiencies.
- Removal of transactions with family or other insiders, such as salary, benefits, and nonmarket (or insider) transactions.
- Implementation of changes in capital structure that could be and perhaps should be implemented, such as incurring reasonable debt when perhaps the family's philosophy has been to avoid debt.

After considering all potential financial statement adjustments and making any appropriate adjustments, your financial statements are ready to use as a basis for the analytical process.

Types of Analytical Analysis

There are two basic types of analysis commonly used to analyze a company's financial and operational performance. They are:

- Common sizing the financial statements.
- Ratio analysis.

Common Sizing

Once financial data has been normalized, analysts commonly employ an analytical methodology to identify operational trends, *common sizing* the financial statements. Common sizing involves expressing each item on the financial statements as a percentage of some base number and is performed on both the normalized balance sheet and the normalized income statement for each period under consideration. On the balance sheet, each item is expressed as a percentage of total assets; on the income statement, each item is expressed as a percentage of sales.

Common-size financial analysis provides insight into the company's historical operating performance, facilitates an assessment of relationships between and among certain accounts, identifies certain trends or unusual items, and can be used to benchmark the operating performance of the subject company by comparing it to its industry or to specific guideline companies.

This analysis is sometimes useful before making normalization adjustments in order to identify other potential adjustments, with a second normalization process then conducted.

A review of historical income statements and common-size income statements illustrate the value of common-size analysis. The historical income statements show the following information for three years ending December 31:

	1st Year	*2nd Year*	*3rd Year*
Net Sales	$128,156,060	$138,267,570	$134,097,420
Cost of Sales	92,261,710	97,934,800	96,185,600
Gross Profit	$ 35,894,350	$ 40,332,370	$ 37,911,820

Without additional analysis, we can conclude:

In year 2, the company made more money (gross profit), than in year 1 because the sales were higher.

The company made less money in year 3 than in year 2 because their sales were lower than in year 2.

We are unable to tell from the raw numbers if there are additional changes taking place in the company that may have positive or negative effects on the company and its long-term future. If we utilize common-size statements for the same financial data, we see the following picture:

	1st Year	2nd Year	3rd Year
Net Sales	100.0%	100.0%	100.0%
Cost of Sales	71.9%	70.8%	71.7%
Gross Profit	28.1%	29.1%	28.2%

From the common-size statements, we are also able to tell that the gross profit deteriorated from the second year to the third year after increasing between the first year and the second year. Obviously, it becomes clear that the cost of sales should be monitored closely to see if additional declines in gross profit could be expected in the future unless the company modifies its operations.

Traveling further down the income statement it is easy to tell that not all the decline in gross profit is attributable to the declining income. Common-size analysis can help the analyst to quickly spot areas that need to be monitored or fixed before they have significant long-term negative effects on the company's value.

Ratio Analysis

Ratio analysis carries the analysis even deeper into the industry and company operational and financial data. The key to ratio analysis is to establish some type of standard or benchmark with which to compare to the company's ratios. For example, if our operational data shows that the company requires five man-hours to manufacture a widget, what does this tell us is useful from a management perspective? Absolutely nothing. However, when it is compared to:

- The historical time required to manufacture a widget, then we know whether our manufacturing process times are improving, declining or staying the same.
- The competition's time to manufacture a similar widget, then we gain the knowledge of whether or not we are likely to be able to improve our manufacturing time without developing some competitive advantage in our manufacturing technology.

The further our company's ratios are from industry standards, the more we should either seek to improve our ratios (operating or financial efficiency) or to maintain or improve our competitive advantage, which created the above-average ratio result.

Ratio analysis exists in two formats: time series analysis and cross-sectional analysis.

Time series analysis (commonly known as trend analysis) compares the company's ratios over a specific historical time period and identifies trends that might indicate financial performance improvement or deterioration.

Cross-sectional analysis compares a specific company's ratios to other companies' or to industry standards or norms. It is most useful when the companies analyzed are reasonably comparable, that is, business type, revenue size, product mix, degree of diversification, asset size, capital structure, markets served, geographic location, and the use of similar accounting methods. It is important to exercise professional judgment in determining which ratios to select in analyzing a given company. Most finance textbooks calculate activity ratios and rate of return ratios based on average beginning and ending year balances. However, much of the available benchmark data, including those from the Risk Management Association (RMA), report ratios based only on a year-end balance.

Exhibits 1.10 and 1.11 present normalized balance sheets and income statements on a common-sized basis, including a comparison with RMA data, respectively.

Comparative analysis is a valuable tool for highlighting differences between the subject company's historical performance and industry averages, pointing out the relative operating strengths and weaknesses of the subject company as compared to its peers, assessing management effectiveness, and identifying areas where the company is outperforming or under performing the industry. Although, every company seems to believe that they are unique and unable to compare themselves to industry data, they must exercise the discipline to use the best available data wherever possible.

Comparative analysis is performed by comparing the ratios of the subject company to industry ratios taken from commonly accepted sources of comparative financial data.

Widely used sources for comparative financial data include:

- Almanac of Business and Industrial Financial Ratios (*www.prenhall.com*).
- BizMiner (*www.bizminer.com*).
- Financial Ratio Analyst (*www.viahome.com*).
- Financial Studies of the Small Business (*www.fvgfssb.com*).
- IRS Corporate Ratios (*www.wiley.com*).
- IRS Corporate Financial Ratios and IRS-CALC (*www.saibooks.com/fin.html*).
- Risk Management Association (RMA) Annual Statement Studies (*www. rmahg.com*),
- Ratios developed from the financial statements of a group of peer companies (normally from publicly traded company's SEC filings).
- Trade Association surveys of member companies.

The preceding publications vary in the depth and breadth of data provided. However, much of the sample data is extracted from corporate tax filings. RMA

Exhibit 1.10   Ale's Distributing Company, Inc.—Comparative Balance Sheets

	RMA 2001	12/31/01	12/31/00	12/31/99	12/31/98	12/31/97
Assets						
Current Assets						
Cash and Equivalents	11.6%	13.0%	13.5%	14.1%	11.1%	13.6%
Accounts Receivable	10.9%	19.0%	16.4%	13.2%	12.1%	10.0%
Inventory	19.7%	20.7%	19.0%	18.1%	18.6%	13.6%
Other Current Assets	2.7%	0.5%	0.9%	1.6%	1.4%	2.3%
Total Current Assets	44.9%	53.2%	49.8%	47.0%	43.2%	39.5%
Fixed Assets-Net*	23.8%	46.8%	50.2%	53.0%	56.7%	60.5%
Intangibles-Net	20.4%	0.0%	0.0%	0.0%	0.0%	0.0%
Other Noncurrent Assets	10.9%	0.0%	0.0%	0.0%	0.0%	0.0%
Total Assets	100.0%	100.0%	100.0%	100.0%	100.0%	100.0%
Liabilities and Equity						
Liabilities						
Current Liabilities						
Accounts Payable	10.9%	2.2%	1.6%	2.5%	1.6%	3.0%
Short-Term Notes Payable	7.4%	0.0%	0.0%	0.0%	0.0%	0.0%
Current Maturity LT Debt	4.4%	0.0%	0.0%	0.0%	0.0%	0.0%
Other Current Liabilities	8.4%	6.0%	6.4%	6.5%	7.0%	6.3%
Total Current Liabilities	31.1%	8.2%	7.9%	9.0%	8.6%	9.3%
Long-Term Liabilities	25.8%	28.1%	28.2%	27.6%	27.2%	26.3%
Other Noncurrent Liabilities	3.7%	0.0%	0.0%	0.0%	0.0%	0.0%
Total Liabilities	60.6%	36.3%	36.1%	36.6%	35.8%	35.5%
Total Equity	39.4%	63.7%	63.9%	63.4%	64.2%	64.5%
Total Liabilities and Equity	100.0%	100.0%	100.0%	100.0%	100.0%	100.0%

Notes: Percentages based on Normalized Historical Balance Sheets.

Subject SIC Code = 5181 (Beer and Ale).

RMA Code = 5181 (Beer and Ale) – $25MM and Over Sales Median Ratios.

*Fixed Assets Adjusted to Fair Market Value.

Source: Reprinted with permission from James R. Hitchner, ed., *Financial Valuation: Applications and Models* (Hoboken, NJ: John Wiley & Sons, 2003), p. 74.

RMA 2001 data from the Risk Management Association, Philadelphia, PA, 2001 (used with permission). © 2002 by RMA—The Risk Management Association. All rights reserved. No part of this table may be reproduced or utilized in any form or by any means, electronic or mechanical, including photocopying, recording or by any information storage and retrieval system without permission in writing from RMA—The Risk Management Association. Please refer to *www.rmahq.org* for further warranty, copyright and use of data information.

Exhibit 1.11   *Ale's Distributing Company, Inc.—Comparative Income Statements*

	RMA 2001	12/31/01	12/31/00	12/31/99	12/31/98	12/31/97
Revenues	100.0%	100.0%	100.0%	100.0%	100.0%	100.0%
Cost of Goods Sold	76.0%	74.4%	74.3%	74.6%	74.4%	73.9%
Gross Profit	24.0%	25.6%	25.7%	25.4%	25.6%	26.1%
Operating Expenses	20.2%	21.9%	22.7%	22.5%	23.1%	21.6%
Operating Profit	3.8%	3.7%	3.0%	2.9%	2.5%	4.5%
Other Income/(Expenses) – Net	–0.5%	–0.1%	–0.1%	0.2%	–0.2%	–0.2%
Pretax Profit	3.3%	3.6%	2.9%	3.1%	2.3%	4.3%

Notes: Percentages based on Normalized Historical Income Statements.

Subject SIC Code = 5181 (Beer & Ale).

RMA Code = 5181 (Beer & Ale) – $25MM and Over Sales Median Ratios.

Source: Reprinted with permission from James R. Hitchner, ed., *Financial Valuation: Applications and Models* (Hoboken, NJ: John Wiley & Sons, 2003), p. 75.

RMA 2001 data from the Risk Management Association, Philadelphia, PA, 2001 (used with permission). © 2002 by RMA—The Risk Management Association. All rights reserved. No part of this table may be reproduced or utilized in any form or by any means, electronic or mechanical, including photocopying, recording or by any information storage and retrieval system without permission in writing from RMA—The Risk Management Association. Please refer to *www.rmahq.org* for further warranty, copyright and use of data information.

obtains its data from financial statements provided to member banks by loan customers. *Financial Studies of the Small Business* obtains small-company financial statements from certified public accounting firms nationwide.

Operational data is much more difficult and usually more expensive to obtain. This data is normally obtained from trade associations or commercial data providers, who are often consulting or accounting firms that work extensively in the particular industry.

Operational and Financial Ratios

When considering both operational and financial ratios there are an almost unlimited number of ratios that can be developed. This section will not present a comprehensive list of all available ratios but rather will include examples of the more common ratios. Financial ratios are generally the first ratios mentioned wherever the topic of ratios is discussed.

Financial ratios are generally broken down into four categories:

- **Liquidity ratios**—Which measure a company's ability to meet short-term obligations with short-term assets. These ratios also help identify an excess or shortfall of current assets necessary to meet operating expenses.
- **Activity ratios**—Also known as efficiency ratios, provide an indication as to how efficiently the company is using its assets. More efficient asset utilization indicates strong management and generally results in higher value to equity owners of the business. Additionally, activity ratios describe the relationship between the company's level of operations and the assets needed to sustain the activity.
- **Leverage ratios**—Which are for the most part balance sheet ratios, assist the analyst in determining the solvency of a company. They provide an indication of a company's ability to sustain itself in the face of economic downturns. Leverage ratios also measure the exposure of the creditors relative to the shareholders of a given company. Consequently, they provide valuable insight into the relative risk of the company's stock as an investment.
- **Profitability ratios**—Which measure the ability of a company to generate returns for its shareholders. Profitability ratios also measure financial performance and management strength.

Exhibit 1.12 shows the typical presentation of the financial ratios organized into these four categories with a short explanation about the use or implication of each ratio.

Although this view of financial ratios is appropriate when limiting your analysis to financial issues, we believe it is an inappropriate view when taking a holistic approach to value creation management. Therefore, the SBfV Model uses an approach that looks at both operational and financial ratios as providing the necessary management information when organized as performance measures around the various tangible and intangible capital resources within the company.

Value Creation Measurement

In addition to performance measures, executive management needs to focus on the company's overall value creation. Is the company's strategy creating value? As discussed earlier, value is represented by the formula:

$$\text{Value} = \frac{I}{R-G} \qquad \begin{aligned} I &= \text{Income} \\ R &= \text{Risk} \\ G &= \text{Growth} \end{aligned}$$

or

$$\text{Value} = \frac{\text{Free cash flow (FCF)}}{\text{Cost of capital (CofC)} - \text{Growth in FCF}}$$

Therefore, value is created when:

- Free cash flow increases,
- Company risk is reduced, or
- The growth rate of the free cash flow increases.

The *Value Creation System* is just what it sounds like and relates to the company's ability to create value. The SBfV Model focuses on the two primary inputs into the value formula: the company's free cash flow and its return on equity. Growth in the company's free cash flow or increases in its return on equity (preferably both) reflects the effects of all management decisions and strategies when compared to its last benchmarking period and shows that the company is creating value. These two performance measures reflect the company's cumulative usage of all its various capital resources. If the company is effectively using its resources, it is creating value and it will be reflected in the company's free cash flow and return on equity improvements.

Free Cash Flow

Free cash flow is the cash that is available to the company's owners after all the cash for the company's internal needs has been committed. These internal needs include cash for capital expenditures, cash repayment of debt, and funds for expansion of the company's operating assets such as inventories and accounts receivable.

Free cash flow is computed as follows:

Start with:	Net income
Plus:	Depreciation, amortization, and other noncash charges
Less:	Incremental working capital needs
Less:	Incremental capital expenditure needs
Plus:	New debt principal added this period
Less:	Repayment of debt principal
Equals:	Free cash flow

Free cash flow, although often provided to management, may be one of the most illusive concepts for management to understand and to project for the future.

Exhibit 1.12 *Typical Presentation of Financial Ratios*

Liquidity Ratios

Liquidity is a measure of the quality and adequacy of current assets to meet current obligations as they come due.

Ratio	*Formula*	*Interpretation*
Current ratio =	$\dfrac{\text{Total current assets}}{\text{Total current liabilities}}$	Rough indication of a firm's ability to service its current obligations. Higher ratios show stronger liquidity; however, the composition and quality of current assets are critical.
Quick ratio =	$\dfrac{\text{Cash + Cash equivalents + Net receivables}}{\text{Total current liabilities}}$	A conservative view of creditors' protection, since inventory and prepaid items may not always be liquid. Generally, a ratio less than 1:1 implies dependency on inventory and other current assets to liquidate short-term debt.
Working capital =	Current assets – Current liabilities	Working capital is a direct indicator of the company's ability to grow.

Efficiency Ratios

Measure the ability to manage working capital, fixed capital, and overall return on invested assets.

Ratio	*Formula*	*Interpretation*
Accounts receivable turnover =	$\dfrac{\text{Credit sales}}{\text{Average accounts receivable}}$	Indicates the number of times it takes receivables to turn into cash per year. Attention should be paid to credit terms, billing procedures, trends, and industry average.
Accounts receivable collection period =	$\dfrac{\text{360 or 365 days}}{\text{Accounts receivable turnover}}$	Reflects average length of time from sale to cash collection.
Inventory turnover =	$\dfrac{\text{Cost of goods sold}}{\text{Average inventory}}$	Indicates the number of times the business liquidates its inventory over a period and whether too little or too much inventory is carried.

(continues)

73

Exhibit 1.12 *(Continued)*

$\text{Inventory} - \text{days in inventory} = $	$\dfrac{360 \text{ or } 365 \text{ days}}{\text{Inventory turnover}}$	Reflects the number of days it takes to sell the inventory. Used in conjunction with accounts receivable collection period to determine operating cycle.
$\text{Operating cycle} = $	$\text{Accounts receivable collection period} + \text{Days in inventory}$	Indicates the length of time it takes to convert inventory to cash. If the cycle increases, more permanent working capital is needed.
$\text{Accounts payable turnover} = $	$\dfrac{\begin{array}{l}\text{Cost of goods sold} \\ - \text{Beginning inventory} \\ + \text{Ending inventory}\end{array}}{\text{Average accounts payable}}$	Indicates the number of turns per period of time it takes for the company to pay its trade payable. Should be compared to credit terms.
$\text{Accounts payable} - \text{days outstanding} = $	$\dfrac{360 \text{ or } 365 \text{ days}}{\text{Accounts payable turnover}}$	Same as above, but expressed in number of days rather than the number of turns.

Ratio	*Formula*	*Interpretation*
$\text{Assets turnover} = $	$\dfrac{\text{Net sales}}{\text{Total assets}}$	Indicates the turnover rate of total assets to achieve net sales. When viewed historically, this ratio indicates the effectiveness of generating sales from asset expansion.
$\text{Net sales to working capital turnover} = $	$\dfrac{\text{Net sales}}{\text{Working capital}}$	An indication of the amount of working capital required to support sales. An increasing ratio may indicate insufficient working capital to support sales growth.
$\text{Inventory to working capital} = $	$\dfrac{\text{Inventory}}{\text{Working capital}}$	Indicates the percentage of working capital supporting inventory. A high percentage indicates operating problems.

Exhibit 1.12   *(Continued)*

Current assets turnover =	$\dfrac{\text{Sales} - \text{Expenses}}{\text{Current assets}}$	Indicates the number of times current assets must turn over to cover expenditures. Measures control of current assets.
Inventory to current liabilities =	$\dfrac{\text{Inventory}}{\text{Current liabilities}}$	Shows the degree to which the company relies on inventory to meet its current obligations.

Profitability Ratios

Profitability ratios measure the operating performance of the business relative to sales, assets, and invested capital.

Ratio	*Formula*	*Interpretation*
Gross profit percentage =	$\dfrac{\text{Gross profit}}{\text{Net sales}}$	Reflects control over cost of sales and pricing policies. The ratio must be viewed in relation to the client's past performance and the industry average.
Operating profit percentages =	$\dfrac{\text{Operating profit}}{\text{Net sales}}$	Indicates the company's ability to control operating expenses. The ratio should be viewed in relation to increased sales and changes in gross profit.
Profit before taxes percentage =	$\dfrac{\text{Profit before taxes}}{\text{Net sales}}$	Provides a more consistent basis for comparisons. It is also used in the calculation of other ratios.
Net income after taxes percentage =	$\dfrac{\text{Net income after taxes}}{\text{Net sales}}$	Reflects the tax impact on profitability and represents the profit per dollar of sales.
Return on equity =	$\dfrac{\text{Profit before taxes}}{\text{Tangible net worth}}$	Measures the return to equity owners and represents their measure of profitability. When compared to the return on assets, this ratio indicates degree of financial leverage.

(continues)

Exhibit 1.12   *(Continued)*

| Return on assets = | $\dfrac{\text{Net income after taxes}}{\text{Total assets}}$ | Reflects the earning power and effective use of all the resources of the company. |

Leverage Ratios

Highly leveraged firms are more vulnerable to business downturns (financial risk) than businesses with less invested capital in the form of debt. Leverage ratios help measure this vulnerability.

Ratio	*Formula*	*Interpretation*
Net fixed assets to tangible net worth =	$\dfrac{\text{Net fixed assets}}{\text{Tangible net worth}}$	Indicates the proportion of net worth that is committed to fixed assets and is not available for operating funds. A low percentage would indicate a favorable liquid position.
Debt to equity =	$\dfrac{\text{Total debt}}{\text{Tangible net worth}}$	Indicates the proportion of debt to total equity that is current in maturity. A high ratio may indicate the need to restructure debt.
Current debt to equity =	$\dfrac{\text{Current liabilities}}{\text{Tangible net worth}}$	Indicates the proportion of debt to total equity that is current in maturity. A high ratio may indicate the need to restructure debt.
Long-term debt to equity =	$\dfrac{\text{Long-term debt}}{\text{Tangible net worth}}$	Measures the relationship of long-term debt to equity.

Coverage Ratios

Coverage ratios measure a firm's ability to service debt.

Ratio	*Formula*	*Interpretation*
Times interest earned =	$\dfrac{\text{Profit before taxes} + \text{Interest}}{\text{Interest}}$	Shows how well the company is able to cover interest from earnings. Measures the level of earnings decline to meet interest payments.
Operating fund to current portion = of long-term debt	$\dfrac{\text{Net income after taxes} + \text{noncash expenses}}{\text{Current portion of long-term debt}}$	Shows the ability of the company to meet its current payments.

Exhibit 1.12   *(Continued)*

Other Ratios

Many ratios compare certain expenses to sales and vary depending upon the industry. Each industry also has certain ratios that measure profitability and productivity. Here are some examples:

Ratio	*Formula*	*Interpretation*
% Depreciation and Amortization to sales =	$\dfrac{\text{Noncash expenses}}{\text{Net sales}}$	Shows the percentage of noncash expenses. Should be compared to cash outflows for capital expenditures.
% Officers/owners salaries to sales =	$\dfrac{\text{Owners' compensation}}{\text{Net sales}}$	Shows the percentage of discretionary salaries paid to owner/managers.

Ratio	*Formula*	*Interpretation*
Net sales per employee =	$\dfrac{\text{Net sales}}{\text{Number of employees}}$	Shows the general efficiency of the work force to generate sales.
Net sales per unit sold =	$\dfrac{\text{Net sales}}{\text{Units sold}}$	An indication of average sales price, per unit, particular to the industry.

Source: Adapted from Financial Ratio Table developed by Darrell V. Arne, CPA, ASA, Arne & Co., Albuquerque, New Mexico, email: *darne@arne-co.com*, website: *www.arne-co.com*.

This is because one of the most difficult aspects of accounting is to understand the relationship between the income statement, the balance sheet, and the cash flow of the business. This is difficult for accountants and even more difficult for the typical business manager. As CPAs working with clients, the standard question we faced when presenting clients with their financial statements was "If I made so much money, how come I have no cash in the bank?"

In the late fifties Lou Mobley became the founding director of the IBM Executive School. He soon discovered that teaching an understanding of the relationship between cash flow and the typical financial statements was one of the major issues he would face in training new managers. Luckily for us, Mr. Mobley went to work on the problem and over the next couple of years developed what has become known as the Mobley Matrix.[28]

He discovered that our normal financial statement presentations are fragmented and that the connections between the various statements are not apparent. Once he had defined the connections.

He developed a one-page columnar matrix showing the beginning balance sheet, the income statement, the cash flow statement, and the ending balance sheet. This index has been called various names since that time, but we still refer to it as the Mobley Matrix.

Mobley's Matrix and its importance can be illustrated by the example of the Sample Widget Manufacturing Company. Exhibit 1.13 shows the balance sheets for the beginning and ending of the calendar year.

Exhibit 1.13   *Widget Balance Sheets*

Sample Widget Manufacturing Company
Balance Sheets for the Periods
($000s)

	(Beginning of Year) January 1	(End of Year) December 31
Assets		
Cash and cash equivalents	$ 25,000	$ 3,000
Accounts receivable	35,000	60,000
Inventory	75,000	105,000
Other operating assets	10,000	0
Notes receivable	0	0
Current assets	145,000	168,000
Gross fixed assets	100,000	120,000
Less accumulated depreciation	(30,000)	(40,000)
Net fixed assets	70,000	80,000
Other investments	30,000	28,000
Total assets	$245,000	$276,000
Liability and equity		
Accounts payable	$ 20,000	$ 32,000
Taxes payable	5,000	3,000
Other liabilities	0	0
Current liabilities	25,000	35,000
Long-term debt	15,000	20,000
Total liabilities	40,000	55,000
Common stock	100,000	100,000
Retained earnings	105,000	121,000
Total equity	205,000	221,000
Total liabilities and equity	$245,000	$276,000

Looking at the beginning and ending balance sheets does very little to help us understand the company's cash flow.

From the balance sheets we can tell:

- Cash decreased by $22,000 and to a very low amount, which implies that the company will run out of cash if it has another year like the past one.
- Accounts receivable increased significantly, but without additional information we cannot tell if sales increased or if management is having trouble with collecting the money owed to the company by its customers.
- Inventory increased, but no indications are given as to why it would increase and what the effects on cash flow would be.
- The company purchased additional equipment that may have had an effect on cash.
- The company purchased more equipment than it depreciated as an expense.
- The company owes significantly more to its creditors than it did in the previous year.
- The company borrowed money but it does not show up in the bank account; there is no sign as to where it went.

The balance sheets provide no indication as to why the company made money but still has no cash in the bank to show for it.

Exhibit 1.14 shows the income statement of the company for the same year. Very quickly, we can see that the company made money for the year, but again the statement does not help us understand why the company has less cash at the end of the year than at the beginning of the year. From the income statement we can tell:

- The company had significant sales and gross profit margins.
- The company had a positive profit before and after taxes.
- The company had very little borrowing throughout the year and ended up with only minor interest expenses and slightly more debt than at the beginning of the year.

Just like the balance sheets, the income statement (which represents the flow between the balance sheets) provides the reader with very little information about why the company has so little cash at the end of the year. Management still cannot answer the basic question "If I made so much money, how come I don't have any money in the bank?"

Exhibit 1.15 shows the cash flow statement for the company for the year.

Exhibit 1.14   *Widget Income Statement*

Sample Widget Manufacturing Company
Income Statement for the Year

Sales	$ 500,000
Cost of goods sold	310,000
Gross profit	190,000
Depreciation	10,000
Goodwill amortization	2,000
Marketing and selling expense	25,000
General and administrative expense	130,000
Operating Income	23,000
Interest and other expense	1,000
Profit before taxes	22,000
Income taxes	6,000
Net profit	$ 16,000

Source: © Copyright 2004 by FVG Holdings, LC and FVG California Partnership. All rights reserved. Used with permission.

With this statement the user can tell how much cash the company collected and where it was used, but it still does not show the relationship between the various accounts on the balance sheets. It still takes a lot of interpretation to tell how the company moved from the beginning of the year balance sheet and the end of the year balance sheet and to understand why the company's cash account may have declined.

Using the Mobley Matrix in Exhibit 1.16 the financial statement user can quickly see the relationships between the various balance sheet accounts and why the cash account has changed for the better or for the worse.

With the Matrix you can account for almost every change that occurs between the beginning and ending balance sheets by adding or subtracting the appropriate numbers from the cash flow statement or the income statement to the beginning balance sheet number. Looking at the Mobley Matrix, the user quickly learns that the various accounts in the cash flow and other statements have been rearranged to have the accounts correspond to the continuity equation relationships between accounts from the left to the right. The first step in the process is to understand the various accounts in each of the statements that relate to each other.

The second step is to understand that the signs (addition or subtraction) will be different on the accounts depending on if you are adding them up vertically or hor-

---

Exhibit 1.15 *Widget Cash Flow Statement*

Sample Widget Manufacturing Company
Statement of Cash Flows
For the Year Ended

Operating Activities	
Collections from customers	$ 475,000
Cash paid to suppliers (inventory paid)	(340,000)
Expenses paid (MSG&A)	(143,000)
Interest and other paid	(1,000)
Prepaid expenses	10,000
Income taxes paid	(8,000)
Cash flow from operating activities (OCF)	(7,000)
Investing Activities	
Fixed asset investment	(20,000)
Other investment	0
Cash flow from investing activities (ICF)	(20,000)
Financing Activities	
Borrow (payback)	5,000
Paid in (paid out)	0
Dividends paid	1,000
Cash flow from financing activities (FCF)	6,000
Increase (decrease) in cash – change in cash	(23,000)
Beginning cash	25,000
Ending cash	$ 2,000

---

izontally. We have included exhibits that demonstrate the math for each of the financial statements.

Exhibit 1.17 shows the vertical math for the income statement. Exhibit 1.18 shows the vertical math for the cash flow statement, and Exhibit 1.19 shows the horizontal math for the Matrix, which connects each of the financial statements.

As an example, look at the income tax account in the cash flow statement (see Exhibit 1.16). The $6,000 is a subtraction (minus) on the vertical math because it uses cash on the cash flow statement and a subtraction on the horizontal math as it reduces the amount of income taxes due on the ending balance sheet.

In contrast, look at the fixed assets on the cash flow statement. The $20,000 is a subtraction (minus) on the cash flow statement because it reduces the cash available, but an addition (plus) on the horizontal math as it increases the assets on the ending balance sheet.

Exhibit 1.16 Mobley Matrix

Sample Widget Manufacturing Company—Mobley Matrix, for the Year ($000)

Beginning Balance Sheet 12/31/XXXX

Cash	$ 25
Accounts Receivable	35
Inventory	75
Other Operating Assets	10
Notes Receivable	0
Gross Fixed Assets	100
Accumulated Depreciation	30
Net Fixed Assets	70
Other Investments	30
Total Assets	$ 245
Accounts Payable	$ 20
Debt	15
Other Operating Liabilities	0
Income Taxes Due	5
Nonoperating Liabilities	0
Stock	100
Retained Earnings	105
Total Liabilities and Equity	$ 245

Income Statement

Sales	$ 500
Cost of Goods Sold	310
Depreciation Expense	10
Intangible Amortization	2
Marketing, Selling, G&A Exp.	155
Interest & Other Expense	1
Income Tax Expense	6
Nonoperating Expense	0
Net Profit	16

Cash Flow Statement

Cash Increase (Decrease)	$(23)
Collections	475
Inventory Paid	340
Prepayments	10
Lend/Receive	0
Fixed Asset Investment	20
Other Investment	0
Expense Paid	143
Borrow/Payback	5
Interest & Other Expense Paid	1
Income Taxes Paid	8
Nonoperating Expense Paid	0
Paid-In	
Dividend & Other Payouts	1
Free Cash Flow	$(22)

Ending Balance Sheet 12/31/XXX

Cash	$ 2
Accounts Receivable	60
Inventory	105
Other Operating Assets	0
Notes Receivable	0
Gross Fixed Assets	120
Accumulated Depreciation	40
Net Fixed Assets	80
Other Investments	28
Total Assets	$ 275
Accounts Payable	$ 32
Debt	20
Other Operating Liabilities	0
Income Taxes Due	3
Nonoperating Liabilities	0
Stock	100
Retained Earnings	120
Total Liabilities and Equity	$ 275

Note: "Prepayments" are a source of funds that are expensed under "Expense Paid".

Source: © Copyright 2004 jointly owned by Chris Mobley, Mobley Matrix International, Inc., and Chuck Kremer.

Exhibit 1.17   *Mobley Matrix Income Statement Vertical Math*

Mobley Matrix
Income Statement
Vertical Math
Top to Bottom

    +   Sales
    −   Cost of goods sold
    −   Depreciation/amortization
    −   Intangible amortization
    −   MSG&A expense
−(+)   Interest and other expense (income)
    −   Income tax expense
    =   Net profit

Source: © Copyright 2004 jointly owned by Chris Mobley, Mobley Matrix International, Inc., and Chuck Kremer. All rights reserved. Used with permission.

Exhibit 1.18   *Mobley Matrix Cash Flow Statement Vertical Math*

Mobley Matrix
Cash Flow Statement
Vertical Math
Bottom to Top

    =   Change in cash
    +   Collections (OCF)
    −   Inventory paid (OCF)
    −   Prepayment (OCF)
    −   Fixed asset investment (ICF)
    −   Other investment (ICF)
    −   Expense paid (OCF)
+(−)   Borrow (payback) (FCF)
    −   Interest and other paid (OCF)
    −   Income tax paid (OCF)
    +   Paid in (FCF)
    −   Dividends and other (FCF)
        OCF   Operating cash flow
        ICF   Investing cash flow
        FCF   Financing cash flow

Note: In this exhibit, the acronym FCF stands for Financing Cash Flow rather than Free Cash Flow as found elsewhere in this book.

Source: © Copyright 2004 jointly owned by Chris Mobley, Mobley Matrix International, Inc., and Chuck Kremer. All rights reserved. Used with permission.

Exhibit 1.19   SBfV Mobley Matrix Horizontal Math

Sample Widget Manufacturing Company
Strategic Benchmarking Scorecard—Mobley Matrix
Horizontal Math (Left to Right)

+	Cash	+ Sales	+ Cash Increase (Decrease)	=	Cash
+	Accounts Receivable	− Cost of Goods Sold	− Collections	=	Accounts Receivable
+	Inventory		+ Inventory Paid	=	Inventory
+	Other Operating Assets		+(−) Prepayments	=	Other Operating Assets
+	Gross Fixed Assets		+ Fixed Asset Investment	=	Gross Fixed Assets
+	Accumulated Depreciation	+ Depreciation Expense		=	Accumulated Depreciation
+	Other Investments	− Intangible Amortization	+ Other Investment	=	Other Investments
+	Accounts Payable	+ Marketing, Selling, G&A Exp.	− Expense Paid	=	Accounts Payable
+	Debt		+(−) Borrow/Payback	=	Debt
+	Other Operating Liabilities	+(−) Interest and Other Expense (Inc.)	− Interest and Other Expense Paid	=	Other Operating Liabilities
+	Income Taxes Due	+ Income Tax Expense	− Income Taxes Paid	=	Income Taxes Due
+	Stock		Paid-in	=	Stock
+	Retained Earnings	+ Net Profit	− Dividends and Other Payouts	=	Retained Earnings

The Matrix also helps us understand the reason that an account such as accounts receivable has changed and its affect on the cash account. If we look at the horizontal math, we find:

Start with:	Beginning accounts receivable	$ 35
Add:	Sales	500
Less:	Accounts receivable collected	475
Equals:	Ending accounts receivable	$ 60

From this analysis, it is easy to see the company sold more than it collected by $25. The $25 uncollected plus the $35 at the beginning of the period, leaves an ending accounts receivable balance of $60.

The same analysis can be performed for every account in the Matrix(see Exhibit 1.19 for an explanation and indication of the Mobley Matrix horizontal math). Inventory is another example of the horizontal math:

Start with:	Beginning inventory	$ 75
Less:	Inventory sold (cost of sales)	310
Plus:	Inventory purchased	340
Equals:	Ending inventory	$105

From this analysis, it can be seen that the company purchased $30 more of products for sale than it used for the actual sales for the year. This $30 is the change in the inventory between the beginning and ending financial statements.

The vertical math for the cash flow statement has changed in that you add the numbers from the bottom to the top (see Exhibit 1.18). The cash account is the very first account and adds horizontally to the ending cash account balance. In contrast, all the numbers add up to the top cash account, which reflects the total change in cash experienced during the period by the company.

The only difficulty to be encountered by the individual filling in the Mobley Matrix is hidden changes to the balance sheets. For these, the user of the financial statements will have to look to the financial statement notes to find the answers. The most common adjustment to the balance sheet will be the disposal of property and equipment. When a piece of equipment is sold, the accountant writes off the asset (credits the accounts) and writes off the accumulated depreciation (debits the accumulated depreciation account).

Any gains or losses, from the sale or disposal of the asset, (the difference be-tween the adjustment to the asset account and the accumulated appreciation ac-count), is the gain or loss recorded on the income statement. These entries made directly to the balance sheet must be accounted for in the Mobley Matrix manually by the preparer of the Matrix.

This Matrix clearly illustrates the relationship between the various financial statements and can be used by all executives regardless of their accounting or fi-nancial management weaknesses. It can be used to analyze historical results or to monitor the cash flow effects of projected management decisions.

Management should be constantly monitoring the current free cash flow and the projected free cash flow to ensure that the decisions they make do not nega-tively affect the company's free cash flows. Short-term drops in free cash flow should only be considered when the present value of the future cash flows is in-creased sufficiently to warrant the temporary, near-term drop in cash flows.

Return on Equity

The second item to monitor to ensure that the company is increasing its value is the return on equity ratio. This ratio is important because it monitors the company's:

- Profitability on sales.
- Effectiveness in the use of its assets (asset turnover).
- Use of leverage or extent of debt financing.

The return on equity (ROE) ratio is computed as:

$$\text{ROE} = \frac{\text{Net income}}{\text{Shareholder's equity}}$$

Clearly, the ratio itself does not directly show the effects of profitability, turnover, and leverage, but if it is broken down into its component parts via the DuPont Formula, the relationship becomes clear.

$$\text{ROE} = \text{Profitability} \times \text{Turnover} \times \text{Leverage}$$

or

$$\text{ROE} = \frac{\text{Net income}}{\text{Sales}} \times \frac{\text{Sales}}{\text{Total assets}} \times \frac{\text{Total assets}}{\text{Equity}}$$

Applying simple algebra, everything cancels out except Net income, which then would be divided by Shareholder's equity, providing our traditional return on equity ratio. The value formula discussed previously uses the company's cost of capital as the denominator.

For public companies, the cost of equity capital is reflected via their stock prices. For private companies, the cost of the equity portion of WACC cannot be computed but must be estimated based on a comparison to the cost of equity of public companies. Because of this difficulty, it is simpler for private companies to use their ROE changes as a proxy for monitoring whether their cost of equity is increasing or decreasing. Although it is necessary to compute an estimate of the company's cost of equity to determine its value, it is not necessary to estimate the cost of equity to determine if the company is increasing its value by decreasing its overall risk or cost of capital.

The SBfV Model uses the ROE as a proxy for monitoring if the company is decreasing or increasing its cost of capital. Because ROE should be managed both historically and on a forecasted basis, good forecasts will help management to understand the effects of their borrowing decisions and the margin for error these decisions allow them. Generally, more borrowing will lower the cost of capital and increase value, that is, use other people's money but only to a point. Pushing the limits and allowing insufficient margins for debt coverage will increase the company's risk and lower its value. Benchmarking within the SBfV Model will allow management the ability to properly manage its debt levels. Managing the company's free cash flow and ROE will ensure that management's overall decisions are increasing the company's value.

Organizing Performance Measures

Selecting the performance measures that are related to a company's critical success factors is the key to effectively managing a company's value through strategic benchmarking. Step three will focus on the concepts of critical success factors and selecting the key benchmarks for your company.

This section highlights some of the key performance measures that may be important to your company. One aspect of selecting your key performance measures is gaining an understanding of the basic ratios and the information they tell about the company. The metrics illustrated are organized by their various capital grouping and by their subgroupings. Subgroups allow management to organize the selected metrics by the type of information provided. They also allow lower-level management, without training in performance measurement, to understand why certain performance measures have been selected.

Physical Capital

Physical capital relates to the company's tangible assets, its plants, machinery, equipment, and technology infrastructure. How management utilizes its physical assets is reflected in many different ratios. These ratios are primarily operational in nature.

Looking at the physical capital as consisting of various resources of the company, they are divided into various categories:

Productive Capacity

These ratios focus on the production that is achieved using the physical facilities and employee base.

$$\text{Sales per employee} = \frac{\text{Annual revenues}}{\text{Full-time equivalent employees}}$$

The higher sales per employee, the higher the profits are that can be realized per employee. This measure is especially used in the software industry but has application in most any industry especially in the service industries.

$$\text{Sales per square foot} = \frac{\text{Annual revenues}}{\text{Square footage used for production}}$$

The higher the sales per square feet of production facility the more usage the company is receiving from its tangible assets. This will minimize the capital investment required to support each dollar of sales and profits.

Investments in Production Assets

These ratios focus on the amount of capital assets that are being purchased or compared to their economic usage as shown by depreciation.

$$\text{Growth in fixed/capital assets} = \frac{\text{Capital expenditures}}{\text{Depreciation expense}}$$

If a company's capital expenditures are significantly higher than its depreciation expense, the company is requiring large amounts of capital to support its operations and growth. As this gap narrows, the company is requiring less capital. This results in higher free cash flows per sales dollar.

There should be periods in the life of every company where depreciation exceeds its capital expenditures. During these periods, the company will be decreasing the amount of capital needed to support operations.

$$\text{Degree of fixed asset newness } = \frac{\text{Accumulated depreciation}}{\text{Gross fixed assets}}$$

Purchasing too much equipment or too little equipment can seriously affect the company. The ratio or degree of fixed asset newness can help management monitor this potential problem. If a company delays updating equipment, its maintenance cost will rise above industry norms and affect profitability. If it purchases too much equipment, it risks creating a negative cash flow, lowering its free cash flow or its profitability. This type of analysis is particularly useful for companies like heavy equipment operators.

Dedication to Maintenance

$$\text{Maintenance costs } = \frac{\text{Maintenance expenditures}}{\text{Revenues}}$$

This ratio focuses on the amount of revenue dedicated to maintaining the company's physical assets (plant and equipment). It is best used as a benchmark against industry averages. Care should be used, as this ratio should increase with the age of the assets. If it is too high, it may indicate the need to invest in new equipment.

Flexibility of Fixed Assets

$$\text{Flexibility } = \frac{\text{Market value of equipment}}{\text{Book value}}$$

This ratio focuses on the market value of the assets compared to their book value. If the market value is lower than the book value, this implies that the company is experiencing more economic depreciation than it has recorded on its financial records. Competitors could replace the company's assets for less than the company has invested and may experience a lower cost of production on their competing products.

Technological Commitment

$$\text{Computer utilization } = \frac{\text{Number of computers}}{\text{FTE employees}}$$

These ratios focus on the company's investments in technology. If they are below industry benchmarks, the company should seriously consider the potential effect of updating its technology and thereby increasing its productivity. This would be accomplished by integrating this analysis with some of the productivity ratios.

Computer utilization should relate specifically to the industry in which the company is engaged. With the proliferation of computer types, networking, and the Internet, the landscape has certainly changed. We now have to consider whether we have smart terminals or fully functional independent robust portables that may or may not be attached to company networks. Consider the impact of the Internet on the ability to file share, or have machine operating manuals online, or a production department troubleshooting a problem online with the machinery manufacturer half the world away. This ratio is becoming more important for both the service and the production industries and can no longer be limited to the administrative functions within the company. Your question is to determine which computers to include in the equation. Does this include the sophisticated cell phones or PDAs or is it limited to full-function laptops or desktops and above?

Software newness = Average age of software applications

Where software companies' business models are so dependent on upgrades for their revenue streams, each customer is forced to balance the cost of upgrades versus the new functionality. Again, industry comparisons may be your best benchmark.

Computing capacity = Average CPU speed per computer
and/or average RAM per computer

This ratio relates to the processing speed of the company's desktop computers. As a company becomes more dependent on processing-intensive applications (graphics, engineering, etc.), this can become a significant productivity measurement.

Access to Suppliers

Logistic ratios = Weighted average distance (by purchase dollars) from suppliers

Two major changes in the United States make this area more critical than in the past. The first is the design of company production schedules that rely more on "on-time delivery." You can stretch your warehousing dollar by relying on the supplier but increase your risks of downtime when weather interferes with the supplier shipments. The second major change is the cost of shipping. Freeways seem to slow transportation efficiency to the point that truckers are not able to predict precise delivery times or costs as fuel costs fluctuate wildly.

Weighted average distance from suppliers is computed by multiplying the total purchase from a supplier by the distance to the supplier. Distance dollars divided

| Exhibit 1.20 | *Weighted Average Distance from Suppliers* | | | | | |

Example A

Miles from Supplier	Total purchases	Distance Dollars
1,000	$ 1,000,000	$ 1,000,000,000
500	1,000,000	500,000,000
100	1,000,000	100,000,000
10	1,000,000	10,000,000
	$ 4,000,000	$ 1,610,000,000
	Weighted Average Distance	403

Example B

Miles from Supplier	Total purchases	Distance Dollars
1,000	$ 500,000	$ 500,000,000
500	750,000	375,000,000
100	1,500,000	150,000,000
10	1,250,000	12,500,000
	$ 4,000,000	$ 1,037,500,000
	Weighted Average Distance	259

by Total purchases equals Weighted average distance from suppliers. This is demonstrated in Exhibit 1.20.

Changing the purchasing strategy by moving your manufacturing facilities can shorten your access to suppliers significantly or:

Logistic ratios = Weighted average (by packaged weight and/or by size) distance from suppliers

If package weight or size is more important, then that should be substituted for the dollars in determining the logistic ratio.

Human Capital

These ratios focus on the quality of the company's workforce.

Education

$$\text{Formal education} = \frac{\text{Total years of education}}{\text{Full-time equivalent (FTE) employees}}$$

This ratio varies widely depending on the industry. Architectural firms could require a substantially higher degree of formal education than a widget manufacturing company. However, no matter what the "Formal education" requirement might be, most companies must provide personal advancement and training expenditures to not only keep their employees at the top of their game but also motivated and stimulated throughout their careers and employment with the company.

Formal education ratio should divide full-time equivalent employees into total years of education. The company must decide what the industry standard is for this ratio. In the United States in the twenty-first century, most employees will have at least an elementary and middle school education. Most employers consider high school as four years, so you have to decide whether a senior in high school is the baseline for your company or whether your employees will have four years of additional education.

$$\text{Personal advancement} = \frac{\text{Educational reimbursement}}{\text{FTE employees}}$$

Some companies encourage their employees to continue their formal education. This can be done through educational reimbursement programs. Usually the employee is reimbursed for the successful completion of each course and not the awarding of a degree. The amount being reimbursed should be divided by, the number of Full-time equivalent employees in the company, division, or department that is being measured.

Training

$$\text{In-house (internal training)} = \frac{\text{Sum of annual internal training hours}}{\text{FTE employees}}$$

Internal training can be a significant component in employee effectiveness and ability to accept more responsibility. Again, the industry standard is important. Some companies have a formal apprenticeship program that combines training and production, but the industry trade groups should be helpful in determining the standard definition of "training." You can easily segregate new employee on-the-job training from more formal company training programs, but as a minimum you should include any training time that requires the employee to be absent from his or her normal workstation or production area.

$$\text{Outside training} = \frac{\text{Sum of annual external training hours}}{\text{FTE employees}}$$

Outside training is similar to the Internal training ratio and usually refers to classes held outside the company by noncompany instructors.

Employee Commitment

$$\text{Absenteeism} = \frac{\text{Average number of sick days per employee}}{\text{Industry average}}$$

One of the most difficult areas to consistently measure is employee commitment. The absenteeism ratio tends to factor in "industry-wide" health characteristics, such as people who work in mines versus those who work in an aerospace company. Usually within an industry, sick days available will tend to be comparable.

$$\text{Sick leave} = \frac{\text{Sick days taken}}{\text{Sick leave available}}$$

The Sick leave ratio is more company specific rather than industry comparable. Depending on the company's written policy, and whether family care is included, this ratio would be a better indicator of employee commitment. Human resources may have policies that make "sick days" difficult to take. One question: Would you rather have an employee stay home with the flu or show up at the company and share his or her germs?

These employee commitment ratios are better used as trend indicators than specific performance indicators.

Trust

$$\text{Employee theft} = \frac{\text{Annual number of employee thefts}}{\text{FTE employees}}$$

In industries that are more prone to inventory and tool shortages (theft), the cost to the company and customers can be significant. Many companies do not have preplanned strategies nor public policies concerning this area and rely on situation-by-situation judgment. The Annual number of employee thefts should reflect the ones where disciplinary action was taken, not presumed "thefts." If this were an area of concern, perhaps Inventory shrinkage or Missing tools per FTE would be a better ratio.

$$\text{Employee complaints} = \frac{\text{Annual number of complaints to HR}}{\text{FTE employees}}$$

Each company should have a system of collecting and categorizing the number of complaints reported to human resources. Although companies with union representation may have a more formal system, any system can be a harbinger of problems that need to be solved before they severely affect customers.

Experience

$$\text{Company experience} = \frac{\text{Total years with company}}{\text{FTE employees}}$$

Human resources should be able to easily determine the total number of years based on their date of hire for each employee. The total years divided by FTE employees, gives us a benchmark of our experience quotient that we can monitor and compare to like companies.

$$\text{Industry experience} = \frac{\text{Total years in industry}}{\text{FTE employees}}$$

A more difficult statistic is "Total years in the industry." Some have maintained that industry experience is crucial to the success of a company; however, there are an equal number of advocates who maintain that "management is management" and a professional manager can transition from industry to industry without significant "startup or industry education on the job training." The debate will rage on with examples of tremendous success by some companies that bring in an outsider to shake things up. On the opposite extreme are colossal failures, where the "knight in shining armor" turned out to be a pile of tin without the mental muscle to win the battle and are relegated to the "executive severance bone yard of failure."

$$\text{Work experience} = \frac{\text{Total years in labor force}}{\text{FTE employees}}$$

Another way of stating this ratio is "Average age of the employee." Although some professions do not really become part of the labor force until years of advanced schooling, internships, and residencies, most do not have those limitations. So, you can divide total ages or Total years in the labor force by FTE employees.

Reputation

$$\text{Survey said} = \text{Overall customer satisfaction rating}$$

The Customer Satisfaction Rating (CSR) is a number that reflects past client satisfaction of the service or products provided by the company. It is calculated by averaging the overall satisfaction scores (on a scale of 1 to 5 with 1 being very dissatisfied and 5 being very satisfied) from the customer satisfaction surveys. The surveys can either be sent after each shipment or service, or periodically at set intervals. The management of the survey process, should be conducted by, an agent independent of the company. The arm's-length process ensures the integrity of the data and the representations.

An alternative to an open survey sent to all customers by an independent firm, is to have top-level executives survey the best or most frequent customers personally. The average rating of these surveys would then be the measure.

$$\text{Repeat customers} = \frac{\text{Sales to repeat customers}}{\text{Total sales}}$$

The Repeat customers ratio is the total sales for a given period of time divided by the total sales. Depending on the company and product this ratio can be computed in a number of ways.

Total sales in dollars to repeat customers divided by Total sales dollars.

$$\text{Repeat customers} = \frac{\text{Transaction to repeat customers}}{\text{Total number of transactions}}$$

You can also use the Number of invoices or transactions to repeat customers divided by the Total number of invoices or transactions.

$$\text{Repeat customers} = \frac{\text{Number of repeat customers}}{\text{Total number of customers}}$$

Initially you might just want to count the number of customers with multiple orders divided by total customers regardless of sales dollars or frequency of orders.

$$\text{Customer longevity} = \text{Average length of customer life}$$

Capturing the date of the first order and the last order date of the customer will allow you to total the days a customer has been using your company. Adding all the cumulative customer order life cycle and then dividing by the number of customers will give you a way of gauging the customer longevity ratio.

Organizational Capital

Product Innovation

$$\text{Average revenue patent } = \frac{\text{Number of patents}}{\text{Total revenue from patents}}$$

Since innovation and new products and services fuel the future growth of the company, you should calculate the Average revenue per patent. Research and development without ultimately having commercially viable products, is usually the realm of academia or funded by grants. In order to reflect an increasing value driver for the for profit business, the ratio of the Total revenue from patents divided by the Number of patents may be an appropriate measure for product innovation.

$$\text{Average revenue per copyright } = \frac{\text{Total revenue from copyrights}}{\text{Total reports for customers}}$$

For a company that provides the service of creating copyrighted reports, the average revenue per copyright is valuable. Revenues from reports must be segregated and totaled then divided by the total number of reports sold.

$$\text{Research and developments percentages} = \frac{\text{Research and development expenses}}{\text{Total company revenues}}$$

Any company that has a research and development budget should at least know the percentage of total revenues that is being spent on the R&D function. How the company determines what to include as R&D expenses is the subject of great debate, but trade association reports may give guidelines to allow company-by-company or industry-by-industry comparisons. At a minimum, the company should at least develop its own definitions in the absence of outside comparisons.

Process Innovation

$$\text{Employee participation } = \frac{\text{Employees making suggestions}}{\text{FTE employees}}$$

Product or process innovation can come from anyone within the company. Often employees not formally involved in R&D or product design can make the most profound contribution regarding new products, product modifications, and process refinements whether for manufacturing or information flow within the company. An example would be a facility maintenance person who overhears a production employee complain about how awkward it is to assemble a product. At night, during the break time, the maintenance crew plays around with some rejected parts and finds that with a small cut here and some lubricant there, everything fits easily. Companies need to not only encourage everyone to think and develop a recognition and reward system but also to capture whether the suggestion system is working.

To make sure that all suggestions do not come from one source it is good to divide the number of Employees making suggestions by the number of Full-time equivalent employees. To further determine the effectiveness of the suggestion system, management can rate the suggestions (on a scale of 1 to 5 with 1 being a suggestion without much merit and 5 being a true innovation). The total score of the combined Employee suggestions divided by the number of suggestions would give the average merit of the suggestions, or if the total score was divided by the FTE employees the ratio would have a different dimension.

Decision Speed

$$\text{Bureaucracy} = \text{Number of organizational levels}$$

Decisions can often be bogged down by the number of approvals they must receive. Although far from perfect, counting the number of organizational levels will give some insight into the potential for bureaucracy.

Perhaps an even better measure would be the average number of employees per level of organization.

$$\text{Bureaucracy} = \frac{\text{Number of FTE employees}}{\text{Number of organizational levels}}$$

Financial Capital

Financial capital is related to the company's use and management of its financial resources. Each of these analytical ratios or calculations help us understand how the business is using its financial resources and how outsiders, such as lenders or investors, perceive the company's management of these resources.

Liquidity

Liquidity reflects a company's ability to meet short-term obligations with short-term assets. These ratios help identify an excess or shortfall of current assets necessary to meet current operating expenses.

Current Ratio

$$\frac{\text{Current assets}}{\text{Current liabilities}}$$

The current ratio is the most commonly used liquidity ratio. Normally, the current ratio of the subject company is compared to industry averages to gain insight into the company's ability to cover its current obligations with its current asset base.

Quick (Acid-Test) Ratio

$$\frac{\text{Cash} + \text{Cash equivalents} + \text{Short-term investments} + \text{Accounts receivable}}{\text{Current liabilities}}$$

The quick ratio is a more conservative ratio in that it measures the company's ability to meet current obligations with only those assets that can be readily liquidated. As with the current ratio, industry norms generally serve as the base for drawing analytical conclusions.

Accounts Receivable Turnover

$$\frac{\text{Annual sales}}{\text{Average accounts receivable}}$$

Accounts receivable turnover measures the efficiency with which the company manages the collection side of the cash cycle.

Days Outstanding in Accounts Receivables

$$\frac{365}{\text{A/R turnover}}$$

The average number of days outstanding of credit sales measures the effectiveness of the company's credit extension and collection policies.

Inventory Turnover

$$\frac{\text{Cost of goods sold}}{\text{Average inventory}}$$

Inventory turnover measures the efficiency with which the company manages the investment and inventory side of the cash cycle. A higher number of turnovers indicate the company is converting inventory into accounts receivable at a faster pace, thereby shortening the cash cycle and increasing the cash flow available for shareholder returns.

Efficiency

Efficiency ratios, also known as activity ratios, provide an indication as to how efficiently the company is using its assets. More efficient asset utilization indicates strong management and generally results in higher value to equity owners of the business. Additionally, activity ratios describe the relationship between the company's level of operations and the assets needed to sustain the activity.

Sales to Net Working Capital

$$\frac{\text{Sales}}{\text{Average net working capital}}$$

Sales to net working capital measures the ability of company management to drive sales with minimal net current asset employment. A higher measure indicates efficient management of the company's net working capital without sacrificing sales volume to obtain it.

Total Asset Turnover

$$\frac{\text{Sales}}{\text{Average total assets}}$$

Total asset turnover measures the ability of company management to efficiently utilize the total asset base of the company to drive sales volume.

Fixed Asset Turnover

$$\frac{\text{Sales}}{\text{Average fixed assets}}$$

Sales to fixed assets, measures the ability of company management to generate sales volume from the company's fixed asset base.

Borrowing Capacity

Leverage ratios, which are for the most part balance sheet ratios, assist management in determining the borrowing capacity or solvency of a company. They provide an indication of a company's ability to sustain itself in the face of economic downturns or to borrow funds to support growth and capital projects. Leverage ratios also measure the exposure of the creditors relative to the shareholders of a given company. Consequently, they provide valuable insight into the relative risk of the company's stock as an investment.

Total Debt to Total Assets

$$\frac{\text{Total debt}}{\text{Total assets}}$$

This ratio measures the total amount of assets funded by all sources of debt capital.

Total Equity to Total Assets

$$\frac{\text{Total equity}}{\text{Total assets}}$$

This ratio measures the total amount of assets funded by all sources of equity capital. It can also be computed as one minus the Total debt to Total assets ratio.

Long-term Debt to Equity

$$\frac{\text{Long-term debt}}{\text{Total equity}}$$

This ratio expresses the relationship between long-term, interest-bearing debt and equity. Since interest-bearing debt is a claim on future cash flow that would otherwise be available for distribution to shareholders, this ratio measures the risk that future dividends or distributions will or will not occur.

Total Debt to Equity

$$\frac{\text{Total debt}}{\text{Total equity}}$$

This ratio measures the degree to which the company has balanced the funding of its operations and asset base between debt and equity sources. In attempting to lower the cost of capital, a company generally may increase its debt burden and hence its risk.

Free Cash Flow to Invested Capital

Start with:	*EBITDA*
Less:	*Taxes*
Plus or Minus:	*Changes in working capital*
Less	*Capital expenditures*
Equals:	*Free cash flow to invested capital*

This reflects the cash flow available to all stockholders, lenders, and equity investors. Positive invested capital to free cash flow demonstrates the company's ability to make a debt payment on any debt it may have or may wish to incur.

Credit Rating

A company's credit rating reflects the outside-world view of the company's worthiness to obtain credit from suppliers and lenders. Difficulties with a company's credit history, capital structure, or profitability (and resulting cash flows) can materially diminish a company's ability to obtain credit.

Profitability

Profitability ratios measure the ability of a company to generate returns for its shareholders. Profitability ratios also measure financial performance and management strength.

Gross Profit Margin

$$\frac{\text{Gross profit}}{\text{Net sales}}$$

This ratio measures the ability of the company to generate an acceptable markup on its product in the face of competition. It is most useful when compared to a similarly computed ratio for comparable companies or to an industry standard.

Operating Profit Margin

$$\frac{\text{Operating profit}}{\text{Net sales}}$$

This ratio measures the ability of the company to generate profits to cover and to exceed the cost of operations. It is also most useful when compared to comparable companies or to an industry standard.

Ability to Raise Equity Capital

Since the capital structure of most companies includes both debt capital and equity capital, it is important to measure the return to each of the capital providers.

Return on Equity

$$\frac{\text{Net income}}{\text{Average common stockholder's equity}}$$

This ratio measures the after-tax return on investment to the equity capital providers of the company.

Return on Investment

$$\frac{\text{Net income} + \text{Interest} (1 - \text{Tax rate})}{\text{Average (Stockholder's equity} + \text{Long-term debt})}$$

This ratio measures the return to all capital providers of the company. Interest (net of tax) is added back since it also involves a return to debt capital providers.

Return on Total Assets

$$\frac{\text{Net income} + \text{Interest} (1 - \text{Tax rate})}{\text{Average total assets}}$$

This ratio measures the return on the assets employed in the business. In effect, it measures management's performance in the utilization of the company's asset base.

Sustainable Growth Rates

Free Cash Flow and Reinvestment

Growth ratios measure a company's percentage increase or decrease for a particular line item on the financial statements. These ratios can be calculated as a straight annual average or as a compound annual growth rate (CAGR) measuring growth on a compounded basis over a specific time period.

Although it is possible to calculate growth rates on every line item on the financial statements, growth rates typically are calculated on such key financial statement items as sales, gross margin, and operating income, and are calculated through use of the following formulas.

Average Annual Sales Growth

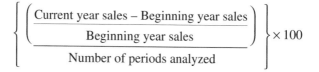

$$\left\{ \frac{\left(\dfrac{\text{Current year sales} - \text{Beginning year sales}}{\text{Beginning year sales}} \right)}{\text{Number of periods analyzed}} \right\} \times 100$$

Compound Annual Sales Growth

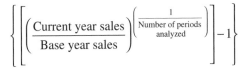

$$\left\{ \left[\left(\frac{\text{Current year sales}}{\text{Base year sales}} \right)^{\left(\frac{1}{\text{Number of periods analyzed}} \right)} \right] - 1 \right\}$$

Average and Compound annual sales growth measures for gross margin and operating income are computed in the same manner. When calculating growth rates on financial statements spread over five years, the typical period used by analysts, the analyst should be careful to obtain growth rates over the four growth periods analyzed. In other words, periods = number of years − 1.

System Capital

Management should look at each of their basic systems within the company as a resource of the company. These systems can vary from the accounts payable system, to a manufacturing process to the information technology infrastructure. Often these systems will overlap and be integrated with each other. These systems can be very strategic assets of a company or simply necessary functions to maintain a competitive position with a competitor.

Dell Computers and Wal-Mart are two companies that have used technology to provide themselves with a competitive advantage. They are both known for their use of technology to run their companies. Dell is known for its systems to provide clients information from ordering a computer to its delivery. It has used the information system to be the lowest-cost provider of computers in the world. Wal-Mart is famous for its use of technology to control its inventory. It monitors everything from the supplier to the customer taking the merchandise from the store. In addition, it allows suppliers to access information about products and thereby increase the efficiency of the product fulfillment delivery systems.

Analysis of each of the company's systems needs to be developed to meet the facts and circumstances for each system. This section will use the information technology system as an example of the type of benchmarking that can be performed for each system.

Plan Analysis

Disaster recovery plan = Disaster readiness index

Every company today should have a disaster recovery plan and an index that is monitored to show its preparedness to recover from a disaster. Most small companies will probably find that they are significantly deficient in their plans for recovery after a disaster. The cost of preparedness is extremely low compared to the cost of losing the company's entire database of company records. The index is a rebased measure where greater than 1.0 exceeds the planned expectations and less than 1.0 is an indication of deficiency. Each component indexed will be a comparison of actual with planned measures. For example, if your plan calls for two sets of computer back-up tapes stored at two different locations but you only have one, the measure for this component is 0.5.

Project management = Projects meeting planned time and expense criteria

The larger the projects being managed and the number of projects being managed, the more the importance of this measure increases. If a company is missing deadlines on a regular basis, the additional cost of capital expenditures and implementing new strategies or client projects can be a disaster for a company.

Response Time

Work request = Fulfillment cycle time

Work-request fulfillment is often a major problem in many companies. Failure to fulfill work requests in a timely manner can lower productivity and create dissatisfaction on the part of employees. We all have experienced the frustration of not getting changes made in a timely manner.

Service calls = Response time

Service calls not returned to employees dependent on their computers creates significant frustrations on the employees' part and can lead to the loss of sales if the individuals cannot access the correct or updated information or properly communicate with customers or the appropriate individual within the firm.

Call waiting = Response time for help desk or service agent to answer calls

Help desk response time is another form of work request or service calls.

Internet = Availability or Average response time

Today the Internet is an extremely important asset for most companies. If the website is not available, or takes too long to provide the information needed by the user, sales or productivity will be lost. Customers will not wait for a slow system but will move on to another supplier of the service or product.

104

Satisfaction

Internal customers (employees/departments) = Satisfaction survey

All of us can testify that we are more dependent on our computers than ever before for information, managing our business, or internal or external communication. We also understand the frustrations of dealing with problems concerning the computers we use. It is extremely important that we monitor the users' satisfaction with the systems we provide them.

External customers = Satisfaction survey

Access of external users to our systems is increasing every day. Their satisfaction will often be the key to increasing our sales or improving our relationships with our suppliers. If the company's sales are dependent on its website, the customers' satisfaction level should be a major management focus.

Help desk = Number of calls per month

The number of calls received by system users is a key indicator of customer satisfaction. If they are not trained in using the system or find it hard to use the system, you can be confident that the satisfaction level is low. If calls are increasing, this is a major problem area to be dealt with. This applies to both internal and external users.

$$\text{Complaints—external system failures or inability to find info} = \text{Number of calls per month}$$

The number of complaints from external users relating to system failures, or the inability to find information on the website, is a strong indictor of customer satisfaction level. Increases in the number of calls or the inability to quickly decrease the number of calls to at least average industry levels should notify management that they have a major problem on their hands that overtime will result in a loss of revenue.

Costs

Capital investments = % change in IT capital investments

As companies become increasingly dependent on technology, changes in the level of capital expenditures reflect a company's ability to maintain its technological edge or failure to implement the new technologies utilized by the competition. With the life of technology assets being so short, significant changes in the level of technology spending will have a greater and quicker impact on the company than changes in the level of spending on long-life assets.

$$\text{Cost per call} = \text{Help desk customer calls/complaints}$$

The cost per call on calls to the help desk or service desk can significantly affect the bottom line of a company. Lowering the cost per call by installing help desk software or by better training of help desk personnel can bring tremendous benefits. Naturally, these benefits are greater the larger number of help desk or service desk personnel the company employs.

$$\text{Infrastructure} = \frac{\text{Number of calls per month}}{\text{Company revenue}}$$

This measure will monitor the load on a company's technology. Systems should be designed for handling a certain number of calls efficiently. As you reach this level and exceed it, you should normally begin to find service problems, increases in the time to handle calls, and decreasing internal and external customer satisfaction.

Customer capital may be the most important capital a company possesses. Anything the company can do to monitor and improve customer-related performance measures will, most likely, result in increased short-term and or long-term revenue.

Customer Capital

Customer Services

$$\text{Availability to customers} = \text{Daily hours available to customers}$$

Availability to customers simply measures the amount of time the company is available to its customers. Management can break this down into additional components, such as office hours, store hours, customer service desk hours, and emergency call hours. Comparing this to the competition's hours will provide additional insight into the company's availability to customers and the potential for lost sales resulting from the competition being available. Sales are lost when the company is not available for the customer's wants, needs, or convenience.

$$\text{Improvements in availability} = \text{Increase in hours available to customers}$$

This measure is related to the previous measure and monitors any changes in the company's availability to the customer.

Effectiveness of customer support = Number of customer calls per month

This measure demonstrates customers' use of the company's support desk and their interest in the company and products. This measure can represent either a positive interest in the product or problems with the product compared to the competition's product. Products designed to require significant personal support are more costly than those that are not. It is also possible for the competition's product to provide a competitive advantage by requiring less support for installation, use, and so forth.

Quality of customer service = Number of customer complaints per month

Unfortunately, the company cannot have all perfect individuals maintaining its customer service or support desks. Therefore, the number of complaints received is an indication that management may need to provide additional training to employees, replace ineffective employees, or add additional employees to cover the incoming customer calls.

Customer Loyalty
Customer life = Average life of customer

The average life of a customer can be of tremendous importance to the company's bottom line. As we all know, it is more costly to obtain a new customer than to support a current customer. Increasing the life of a customer is extremely important to the company. If the average life of a customer is decreasing, then management should expend the effort to investigate the reason. Drops in the life of a customer generally indicate future problems or declines in revenue, cash flow, and return on equity. The causes for a drop in the life of a customer can range from new technology replacing the product, to decline in the product's quality, to problems with the company's sales force.

Sales per customer = Average purchase per customer

Changes in the average dollar purchases of a customer can also indicate an expected future increase or decrease in a company's profits and cash flows. If the company is experiencing a decline in the average dollar amount purchased, it very well may be reflecting a drop in the customer's loyalty to the company and its products or services.

The average sales per customer should be tracked on a monthly, quarterly, and annual basis. Changes in the level of purchases by a particular customer may be important for large customers, but often the average sales for a group of small customers may be more important than those for any one of them in particular. The small customers can be monitored by geographic region, type of customer, or any other appropriate criteria.

$$\text{Customer satisfaction} = \text{Customer satisfaction survey}$$

Surveys are an important means of monitoring a customer's satisfaction level. Although dissatisfaction may not have resulted in a current loss of sales, it can be an indicator of expected future loss of customers as soon as they encounter a suitable alternative for your product or service. If the customer is unsatisfied, they are most likely looking for a replacement product or provider, or at a minimum, they will be receptive to alternative providers or products.

$$\text{Market Penetration Customer retention} = \text{Customer defection rate}$$

Every company or service provider will lose customers or referral sources. The rate of defection is the performance measure to be monitored. If a company is experiencing an increasing defection rate or if the current rate is higher than the competitors', it will be more difficult for the company to maintain its profit margins or to gain new customers. Customers who leave a company are more likely to tell their friends why they left than those who stay are to tell their friends why they use a company's services or products.

$$\text{Dollar penetration} = \text{Total market share} - \text{dollars}$$

Dollar market share demonstrates the portion of the total market controlled by the company. But this measure alone is not enough. High-ticket items in the category will pick up a disproportionate share of the dollar penetration. Although the company has the market penetration based on dollars, a low-priced product with a high unit penetration could begin to move upscale and begin to eat into the company's market share without the company being aware of the true issues.

$$\text{Customer penetration} = \text{Total market share} - \text{Customers}$$

Customer share is also a key factor. Every company needs to control as many of the potential customers as possible. The customer base allows the company to sell additional products or services to each of the customers. If a company does not control the customers, the competition will.

$$\text{New customers} = \text{New customers per month}$$

The only way to increase the company's market share is to be constantly adding new customers at a rate greater than the competition. Without this number, it is impossible to determine the cost to obtain a new customer. Budgeting for marketing expenses and determining the effectiveness of marketing programs is dependent on this number as part of the analysis process.

$$\text{Customer penetration} = \text{Average number of products sold per customer}$$

Customer penetration really relates to the number of products sold to each individual customer. If a company can improve this average per customer, sales will increase without the cost of adding new customers.

Website
The effectiveness of the company's website is highly dependent on the usage of the website by the various users. To determine the site's effectiveness a variety of measures must be considered at a minimum.

Website Information Access

$$\text{Customer usage} = \text{Number of customers/total customers}$$

The most effective measure is to determine the portion of the company's current customers that use the website. This would be dependent on the number of unique users not the number of times a customer used the site. The more the company is able to entice the customer base to use the website, the more it can lower marketing costs and provide focused information to its customers.

$$\text{Frequency of usage} = \text{Internet sessions per active customer}$$

The frequency of usage by the individual customers allows the company to continue the refinement of the analysis of the effectiveness of the website. The more frequently the customers use the website the easier it is for the company to provide personalized service and information to these same customers.

$$\text{Amount of usage} = \text{Length of session per visitor}$$

The length of the average session per user also is an additional refinement of the effectiveness analysis. The more a customer uses the site the more he or she becomes dependent on the site and the company for information on products or services. Declining usage of the site may indicate that it is time for a major overhaul of the company's website.

$$\text{Ease of completing purchases} = \text{Percentage of online purchases terminated in process}$$

This measure is extremely important to management because it indicates the site's effectiveness in closing the sale. It is estimated that for some companies, up to 65 percent of the customers who start the online sale process never complete the sale. The reasons range from complexity of the process to the fact that the computer terminated the sale for no apparent reason at all.

This number has probably decreased as the design of online stores has continued to evolve and companies have improved the performance of their online commerce capabilities. Management must continue to monitor its performance in this critical area as the number of purchase transactions completed online continues growing at an astonishing pace.

NOTES

1. Michael Porter, "How Competitive Forces Shape Strategy," *Harvard Business Review* (May–June 1979), pp. 137–145.
2. Michael Porter, *Competitive Strategy: Techniques for Analyzing Industries and Competitors* (New York: Free Press, 1980).
3. Michael Porter, "How Competitive Forces Shape Strategy," *Harvard Business Review* (May–June 1979), pp. 137–145.
4. *Ibid.*
5. Robert H. Waterman, Jr., Thomas J. Peters, and Julien R. Phillips, "Structure Is Not Organization," *Business Horizons* (June 1980), pp. 14–26.
6. *Ibid.*
7. Adapted from Liam Fahey and V.K. Narayanan, *Macro Environmental Analysis for Strategic Management* (St. Paul: West Publishing, 1986), p. 29; and from Michael A. Hitt, R. Duane Ireland, and Robert E. Hoskisson, *Strategic Management: Competitiveness and Globalization*, 3rd ed. (Cincinnati: South Western Publishing, 1999), pp. 50–60.
8. Michael Porter, *Competitive Strategy: Techniques for Analyzing Industries and Competitors* (New York: Free Press, 1980).
9. *Ibid.*
10. *Ibid.*
11. *Ibid.*
12. *Ibid.*

13. *Ibid.*
14. *Ibid.*
15. *Ibid.*
16. *Ibid.*
17. *Ibid.*
18. *Ibid.*
19. Malaspina University-College website: *http://planning.mala.bc.ca/primer/primer. asp?title=definition7&section=2).*
20. Hill & Westbrook, "SWOT Analysis: It's Time for a Product Recall," *Long Range Planning*, Vol. 30, No. 1 (1997), pp. 46–52.
21. *Ibid.*
22. Christopher Hart, *Extraordinary Guarantees: Achieving Breakthrough Gains in Quality & Customer Satisfaction* (AMACOM, May 1993).
23. Raef Lawson, William Stratton, and Toby Hatch, "The Benefits of a Scorecard System," *http://ww.managementmag.com/index.cfm/ci_id/1457/la_id/1, CMA Management* (June 2003).
24. Bullen and J .F. Rockert, "A Primer on Critical Success Factors," Center for Information Systems Research Working Paper No. 69, Sloan School of Management, M.I.T., Cambridge, MA.
25. Dr. Sheila Kessler, "Benchmarking: A New Consulting Service for CPAs," *Competitive Edge* (1999).
26. *Ibid.*
27. Jay B. Barney, *Gaining and Sustaining Competitive Advantage* 2nd ed. (Reading, MA: Addison-Wesley Publishing, 2002), p. 156.
28. The Mobly Matrix©, referred to in this text as the Financial Scoreboard©, is protected by a compilation copyright jointly owned by Chris Mobley, Mobley Matrix International, Inc., and Chuck Kremer. The use in this book of the Mobley Matrix is in no way a waiver of the owners' compilation (software development) copyright property rights in the material.

STEP 2

Desired Future State

FUTURE STATE

The second step in the SBfV process is documenting management's vision of its company in the future and what it takes to accomplish it. Today's owners and managers must describe their company's future state. All managers have a vision of their company, but not all of them have described that vision on paper. Management must describe its vision of the company in the future and then determine what is required to achieve that vision. Management needs to answer specific questions covering the entire function of the company to describe the vision. Some of the questions to ask might be:

- What is management's vision of what the company will look like in five or ten years?
- Will it be a 10-million-dollar company or 10-billion-dollar one? Perhaps the measure should be number of stores or distribution centers.
- In what markets will the company be a leader?
- Will these markets be local, regional, national, or global?
- What will the market penetration level be?
- What products or services will be sold?
- Will the company's current products or services get the company where it wants to go?
- How many employees will be needed?
- Will more automation be required?
- Will the current capital structure be sufficient?
- Will the company remain private or go public?
- Will the company's current strategy get it where it wants to go?
- Do the company's critical success factors support its strategy?
- Does the company have the necessary resources to achieve its future state?

The analysis should center on identifying the core business strategy that will be required to achieve the vision for the company. In addition, management should focus on the company's core products or services, its long-term business goals, the critical success factors (CSFs) necessary to carry out the core strategy, and the key performance indicators (KPIs) for each critical success factor. We have already discussed each of these components separately but not in the context of the Future State. Therefore, this will be a relatively short chapter.

CORE STRATEGY

As we discussed earlier, Michael Porter in his book *Competitive Strategy* outlined three generic strategies that today's owners and managers must choose from to develop their business strategy. If they do not select one of the strategies and focus on it over the long term, they will not be effective and will find themselves in the ineffective state he refers to as being "stuck in the middle." The three strategies are:

- Overall cost leadership, also called Operational Excellence.
- Differentiation from competitors, also called Product Leadership.
- Focus on a particular buyer group, segment of the product line or geographic area, also known as Customer Intimacy.

Each of these strategies requires the existence of certain characteristics related to common skills, resources, and organizational requirements. The basic concept is that the resulting strategic position will provide the company with above-average returns in the industry despite having strong competitors. These three strategies are the core of the SBfV Model.

But to review, overall cost leadership (Operational Excellence) as a strategy requires management to pursue a course of action that aggressively works to reduce all costs yet does not allow actions to negatively affect quality, customer service, or new product development. Differentiation from competitors (Product Leadership) requires management to create something that is perceived industry-wide as being unique. This strategy allows premium pricing over the competition due to the brand loyalty of the customers. Generally, this strategy precludes the company from obtaining a high market share and often is associated with the concept of exclusivity. Products tend to be more costly due to the product design requirements, the additional research and development required, the high-quality materials used, and the level of customer service provided. And finally, the third strategy, focus on a particular buyer group, segment of the product line, or geographic area (Customer Intimacy) and is based on being able to serve a highly focused target group more effectively or efficiently than the company's competitors. The competitors are assumed to be marketing to a more diverse market, either across a larger geographic market or with a broader product line.

Each of these three strategies needs a very different style of leadership and generally evolves into a unique corporate culture. In addition, each of these strategies requires the use of different performance measures. Being the low-cost provider would necessitate a focus on performance measures related to manufacturing, while a strategy based on differentiation would focus on performance measures related to customer satisfaction and perceptions. Although all companies follow one of the three generic strategies, unless they find themselves "stuck in the middle," the strategies are developed uniquely by each company based on their marketplace and resources.

The development by management of its company's specific core products and related long-term goals must be reconciled with the core strategy. Once management has set the parameters for the strategy, has decided what it does well, and has established its long-term goals (internal ones such as growth and external ones such as community service), then it is time to establish the related critical success factors.

The core strategy includes decisions related to core products and long-term goals that must be decided in light of the risk borne by the company. Management must understand its industry in order to best determine its own strategy. The Porter Model is used to analyze and assess company risk associated with industry structure[1] by dividing industry structure into five forces:

1. Rivalry between current incumbents
2. Threat of new entrants
3. Bargaining power of customers
4. Bargaining power of suppliers
5. The threat of substitute products

Further removed from the subject company than industry forces but still affecting it significantly, are five macroenvironmental sources of risk:[2]

1. Technological risk
2. Sociocultural risk
3. Demographic risk
4. Political risk
5. Global risk

A key to analyzing the company's future state is understanding the company itself and how it relates to the industry and the macroenvironment it operates in. Management must figure out what the company does well and then must set out to do that thing very well.

CRITICAL SUCCESS FACTORS

Every business has critical success factors that will increase revenue, reduce costs, or increase efficiencies. Management can define or discover the critical success factors of the company for every performance area in the company. The definition of critical success factors (CSFs) presented in Step 1, and the one we believe provides the best insight for those trying to understand CSFs, bears repeating:

> Critical success factors are the limited number of areas in which satisfactory results will ensure successful competitive performance for the individual, department, or organization. Critical success factors are the few key areas where "things must go right" for the business to flourish and for the manager's goals to be attained.[3]

Identifying "those things that must go right" is one of the primary responsibilities of management. Depending on the strategy the company has chosen, the CSFs will vary even within the same market. Based on our experience, we believe that a CSF has the following characteristics, which management can consider when developing their own CSFs:

- Has a material impact on the bottom line and strategic effectiveness,
- Directly affects successful competitive performance of company,
- Is usually one of less than 10 factors in any one company,[4]
- Most likely affects customer satisfaction, directly or indirectly, or
- Must be related to the company's strategy.

We agree that there are probably less than 10 critical success factors for any business. This is especially true the smaller the company. Even if there were more than 10 CSFs in small to midsized businesses (SMBs), these companies would not have the management depth to focus on more than a few CSFs at any one time. Management responsible for SMBs may need to occasionally change the primary focus of the performance measurement system, which would allow a rotating emphasis year by year between major themes.

KEY PERFORMANCE INDICATORS

Every critical success factor has various performance indicators that affect it. Since management can only manage a limited number of items, it is important to select the most important performance indicators for each CSF, called key performance indicators (KPIs). KPIs have unique characteristics that management must consider when selecting them. Each indicator:

- Relates to a specific procedure or process.
- Is an input item for a specific performance indicator.
- Must have consistency of measurement.

The art of selecting KPIs requires that management understand how the CSFs and their KPIs are significant components of the company's corporate strategy. If the KPIs or benchmarks do not support the strategy, management will not be effective in advancing the company's market position, ROE, cash flow, or resulting value.

BENCHMARKING

In some ways, benchmarking is a never-ending process. Management is always looking for better and cheaper ways to do things. Benchmarking provides a format for that search. It focuses on better practices for more productivity (see "SBfV's Five Dimensions of Value"). Benchmarking can be derived internally or externally. Internal benchmarks would be baseline measures (orders, units produced, operating expense ratios, etc.) or best units or people (saleswoman of the month, product line profitability, etc.).

External benchmarking gets a little tricky. Everyone and every company wants to find the Holy Grail: What is the target of the best and the brightest? Well, here is a clue: It does not exist! Oh, there are external marks to be sure, but no external marks that specifically reflect the facts and circumstances of your company. Transferring a specific external benchmark to your company is like transplanting a Mensa brain into your body. It simply will not work. Nevertheless, external marks are useful aids to management in selecting its targets. They come in a variety of types such as competitive marks from industry sources (JD Powers, Risk Management Associates), recognized best practices from trade associations, and strategic benchmarks to achieve some specific strategy. Ultimately, management has the responsibility to decide which is best. As long as such decisions are made within the grand strategy, and particularly within the SBfV Framework of the Six Levels of Capital (customer capital, systems capital, financial, human, organizational, and physical capital), management's decisions will be effective.

Benchmarks can be set in one of four ways:

1. Maintain the current level of performance.
2. Set the mark against an internally desired level of performance.
3. Set the mark against an industry level of performance.
4. Set the mark against a specific peer group's level of performance.

The benchmarks need to be reviewed and adjusted annually or upon the occurrence of a specific triggering event (addition of new equipment, etc.). Adjustments should be made cautiously, with realistically achievable improvements in mind.

Identifying CSFs

Prioritization and development of consensus is essential to identifying and managing CSFs. Obviously, the CSF must be aligned with the corporate strategy, but usually the existence of a strategy is not the problem. The execution of the strategy through the CSFs and KPIs is. More on this in Step 4, but for now we will restrict ourselves to the important tools available, which will not only identify the CSFs and KPIs but also create appropriate buy-in through the facilitation process.

There are a number of tools available to identify a range of options and build consensus. Our favorite is the Paired Comparison Analysis. This tool is best defined in an article by Marsh and Bergman:

> Paired Comparison is a powerful voting, prioritization and consensus technique. It can be used by an individual, but is more commonly used by a team, to prioritize a range of options or root causes (those vital and systemic for improvement). By comparing each option with every other option, scores and rankings are created. The degree of consensus in the team can be explored by producing histograms of the scores for each option. Areas of disagreement can then be focused on.
>
> Paired Comparison is a subjective, opinion based technique. It is used in the absence of hard data, where precise cause and effect linkages are difficult to measure and when dealing with feelings and opinions. It is not a substitute for data collection and data analysis.
>
> Typical applications include: identifying the 'critical few' root causes, prioritizing factors for success and prioritizing possible solu-

tions. In fact it is applicable whenever consensus needs to be achieved concerning a number of options. [5]

Paired Comparison Analysis is essentially a matrix of options put to a Likert scale[6] (as in "disagree," "somewhat agree," etc.). The downside to the process is that the design matrix (the potential options related to the critical business process) can get quite large. There is a technique for handling this related to Poisson loglinear models and Iterative Weighted Least Squares (IWLS) algorithms. Hatzinger and Francis addressed this in "Fitting Paired Comparison Models in R," the abstract for which reads:

> Paired comparison models in loglinear form are generalized linear models and can be fitted using the IWLS algorithm. Unfortunately, the design matrices can become very large and thus a method is needed to reduce computational load (relating to both space and time). This paper discusses an algorithm for fitting loglinear paired comparison models in the presence of many nuisance parameters which is based on partition rules for symmetric matrices and takes advantage of the special structure of the design matrix in Poisson loglinear models. The algorithm is implemented as an R function. Some simple examples illustrate its use for fitting both paired comparison models and (multinomial) logit models.[7]

The article is recommended reading only for the avid and mathematically inclined. For those who are practical and application oriented, visit *www.mindtools.com*, which presents a number of other tools for decision making, including Grid Analysis and Six Thinking Hats. Each of these tools provides a process for stratifying the relative importance of subjective factors.

Figuring out the Future State of your company requires vision, patience, execution, facilitation, and buy-in at the grassroots level. The Future State cannot be dictated; it cannot be decided on and then approached as, "Let's inform the masses." Experienced facilitators will use controlled processes, ask questions, hold workshops, encourage free-flowing exchanges, and provide frank feedback to owners and managers. The identification process takes time, the buy-in takes longer, and the execution of cultural change takes the longest time. For a company with, say, 1,000 employees, the identification and buy-in may take a year and the cultural change two or three years. Let's face it, such a company may have taken 20 years to get where it is; it is going to take some time to change the direction of that ship.

NOTES

1. "Michael Porter, "How Competitive Forces Shape Strategy," *Harvard Business Review* (May–June 1979), pp. 137–145.
2. Adapted from Liam Fahey and V. K. Narayanan, *Macroenvironmental Analysis for Strategic Management* (St. Paul: West Publishing, 1986), p. 29; and from Michael A. Hitt, R. Duane Ireland, and Robert E. Hoskisson, *Strategic Management: Competitiveness and Globalization*, 3rd ed. (Cincinnati: South Western Publishing, 1999), pp. 50–60.
3. Sheila Kessler, *Benchmarking: A New Consulting Service for CPAs* (San Clemente, CA: Competitive Edge, 1999).
4. *Ibid.*
5. John Marsh and Todd Bergman, *Using Paired Comparisons to Achieve Consensus*, http://www.tarrani.net/.linda/pairedexplained.pdf.
6. Rensis Likert (1903–1981), *"A Technique For The Measurement of Attitudes"* (1932). One product of this study was the creation of what would become the most widely used scale for attitude measurement, the Likert scale. Structurally, this attitude scale is anchored by two extremes, ranging from favourable to unfavourable, with a neutral midpoint for each statement.
7. Reinhold Hatzinger and Brian J. Francis, "Fitting Paired Comparison Models in R," Department of Statistics and Mathematics Wirtschaftsuniversitat Wien, Research Report Series, Report 3 (May 2004) website: *http://statistik.wu-wien.ac.at/*.

STEP 3

Strategic Benchmarking Keys

HOW STRATEGY ALIGNMENT BUILDS VALUE

Strategy Overview

Strategy is a word tossed around in most companies. Strategic study groups are formed. Strategy development support teams are constituted. Costly consultants are engaged, and hours are spent in planning and drafting strategic plans.

Unfortunately, it appears that only 10 percent to 30 percent of companies are successfully able to execute their strategies. Moreover, further studies by Kaplan & Norton show:

- Only 5 percent of the workforce understands their company's strategy.
- Only 15 percent of senior management teams spend more than one hour per month discussing strategy.
- Only 25 percent of managers have their compensation tied to strategy.
- Only 40 percent of organizations link their budgets to strategy.[1]

Most companies do not have the strategic alignment tools to effectively and efficiently execute their strategies, leverage their support systems, and optimize their peoples' competencies in order to sustain growth and productivity for the long run. In this section, we will explore the Strategic Benchmarking for Value (SBfV) Process to show how it can successfully align any company to build value. We will focus on our *Return on Strategy Execution* (ROSE), within the SBfV Framework of return on equity and free cash flow discussed earlier.

GRAND STRATEGY, STRATEGY, OR TACTICS?

Is there a difference or is this just semantics at play? Grand strategy provides the purpose and guidance to all lower-level strategy and tactics. It has great merit and application in the corporate world. If a corporate leader allows too much focus on lower-level strategy and tactics, a disproportional amount of effort and resources will be spent on short-term objectives. If so, your company may only realize a short-term victory, and you will not be able to sustain long-term outcomes.

So how does a corporate leader create a strategic situation or condition in the marketplace so advantageous that the very condition brings about favorable long-term decisions and desired outcomes? Simply stated, but often not committed to—he or she labors over developing, framing, communicating, integrating, driving, resourcing, and measuring the performance of an enterprise-wide grand strategy. Corporate leaders who fail to recognize this reality do so at great risk to their company and career.

Today, a corporate grand strategy should be framed out analogously to how military strategy is shaped from cited national interests and national security strategic perspectives. Some refer to this as an *Enterprise-Wide Strategy*. The grand strategy paints the picture of the Future State that the company wants to create in the marketplace, which will enhance the company's strategic position and economic profits. Enterprise-wide strategy needs to be balanced with long-term goals and short-term activities. An effective enterprise-wide strategy will:

- Clearly articulate cause-and-effect linkages between input activities and desired outcomes.
- Describe a company's recipe for success—the ideal combination of WHATs with the HOWs.
- Logically link and align intangible assets and their associated contributory, tangible assets.
- Serve as the instrument against which leadership can prescribe and prioritize the apportionment of effort in the face of high residual uncertainty.
- Serve as the instrument to align all reporting units and tactical action systems capabilities with people's knowledge requirements and competency development.
- Serve as the instrument to drill strategic intent down to each business unit so lower-level decisions, strategy, and tactics can be developed and implemented.
- Serve as the one instrument that will coordinate and direct the resources of the company toward the attainment of the defined strategic objective of the business—the goals defined by fundamental policy.

- Serve as the instrument to align and prioritize budgets and operational plans.
- Be structured for continuous adaptation to rapidly changing economic and market environments.
- Provide a line-of-sight focus and direction for everyone in the company.
- Be easy to understand and continually communicated throughout the company.
- Be the organizational alignment tool to modify behaviors and change cultures.

Most importantly, enterprise-wide strategy execution cannot be delegated to planning committees. It is the leader's responsibility to oversee and drive the strategy vertically and horizontally throughout the company. Hamel and Prahalad refer to Strategy as "Stretch and Leverage" and recognize the paradox of competition: "leadership cannot be planned for, but neither can it happen without a grand and well-considered aspiration."[2] They refer to the term *strategic intent* as "strategic architecture's capstone." Enterprise-wide strategy purposefully implies a significant stretch for the company. SBfV's grand strategy entails the same by providing a company with a defined Future State that is the foundation of strategy alignment. It is not something that is added to leadership's plate—it is the plate.

TRANSLATING GRAND STRATEGY INTO STRATEGY EXECUTION

Grand strategy is the art and science of employing the Six Levels of Capital (customer, systems, financial, human, organizational, financial) to affect the maximum support of adopted policies. It involves determining what need or demand we must respond to and how we will respond to achieve the desired future for the company. It is the glue that holds decision makers and all six levels of capital in alignment and moving in the same direction. Successful leadership today is grounded in a deep understanding and operational appreciation for the power of executing effective strategy. Again, the operative word here is executing. Studies show that between 10 percent and 30 percent of corporate strategies effectively formulated are effectively executed.[3] That leaves somewhere between 90 percent and 70 percent of the most critical value-building instruments on a shelf or in some fancy binder.

Real value building occurs in companies when leadership, sometimes unknowingly, practices operational art. Operational art or *operations* refers to an intermediate field of study and practice between the strategic and the tactical levels. Tactics alone cannot accomplish strategic objectives; results of tactical actions are useful only when linked together as a part of some larger design framed by strategy and orchestrated by Operational Art. The gap between strategy and tactics is too large to be bridged without an intermediate field of study and the practice of operational art.

Corporate leaders who practice operational art translate grand strategy into operational objectives that can be achieved predominantly by tactically controlled resources at the reporting or business unit levels. SBfV is an effective process to infuse the practice of operational art into the corporate environment.

Principles of Corporate Strategy

In his book, *Principle-Centered Leadership,* Steven Covey asserts that throughout history leaders have employed models and maps to reinforce their decisions on the management of people and systems to foster greater productivity.[4] These models varied from the old "carrot-and-stick" approach to more comprehensive models based on influence strategies and advanced systems capabilities. However, Covey goes on to point out that in this complex, dynamic world, core business quality measures can become obscured. "We confuse efficiency with effectiveness, expediency with priority, imitation with innovation, cosmetics with character, or pretense with competence."[5] Leaders need to teach and be guided by a set of proven "principles" in their companies as an enlightened approach to management and leadership. These principles are natural laws and governing values that have survived every great society and every responsible civilization throughout history. Covey refers to these principles as a compass that always points the correct way— true north is always true north no matter where on the business map we are presently located. These principles are characterized as:

- Self-evident and self-validating.
- Unchanging (even though uncertainty and turbulence characterize most organizations today).
- Applying at all times in all places for all organizations.[6]

These are the *principles of corporate strategy* which, if followed, will always tend toward success in battle, and with equal assuredness, if neglected or ignored, will tend toward defeat or even destruction.

SBfV's PRIDE Principles

SBfV advocates the PRIDE principles to sustain organizational competitiveness:

1. Proactive strategies
   a. Issues clear, focused, well-communicated strategies.
   b. Guide clarity of purpose, direction, focus, and speed.

  c. Determine who holds the market "high ground" and sets competitive decision cycles.

  d. Proactive strategies are "shaping" strategies, not reactive. They are forward looking and focused on shaping future markets as opposed to reacting to market shifts.

  e. Tactical offensive initiatives are still reactive strategies. They are based on more predictable events in a shorter time frame with less uncertainty prevailing.

2. **Resource alignment to strategy**

  a. Develops a resource based on the Six Levels of Capital for a strategic and performance-based organizational culture.

  b. Guide systems capital and human capital with resulting unity of effort in competency development and application.

  c. Tangible assets determine capability.

  d. Intangible assets determine potential and readiness.

  e. Optimal tangible and intangible combinations prioritized against and aligned with strategy will produce optimal economic profits.

3. **Innovative and adaptive**

  a. Develops a less hierarchical and more flexible organizational structure.

  b. Determines competitive advantage in managing complex adaptive systems.

  c. Differentiates products, process, and market leadership.

  d. Determines cycle time and speed to market.

  e. Determines ability to adapt to changes in a projected operational environment.

  f. Protects against competitive advantage losses and intellectual capital giveaways.

4. **Defined future core business**

  a. Ensures that there is absolute clarity throughout the company about goals and objectives.

  b. Defines growth objectives.

  c. Pulls strategy to the preferred Future State of the business.

  d. Clearly articulated and simple to comprehend.

  e. Provides clear line of sight and understanding of personal fit throughout the company.

5. **Effectiveness with efficiency**

  a. Displays excellent operational execution.

b. Ensures the right stuff is used in support of the right objective at the right time the right way.

c. Affects overall organizational competitiveness, sustainability, and bottom line.

d. Has to be measured.

Do the PRIDE principles really apply to companies today, or is this just some cute cliché? In Harvard Business Online's October 2003 *Management and Strategy Alert*, the results of a 10-year study analyzing 200 different management practices were released assessing which practices really make a difference to the bottom line. The analysis found, ". . . there appears to be no meaningful link between most practices and long-term performance." "Our analysis found connections with shareholder return extremely rare."[7] The study included assessments of such highly touted practices as: (1) Enterprise Resource Planning (ERP), (2) Customer Relationship Management (CRM), (3) 6-Sigma, and (4) corporate governance.

The researchers found great inconsistencies between highly profitable and less profitable companies in the quality of execution and the persistence in using the adopted practice to actually drive performance throughout the organization. They found that successful companies vigorously adhere to, albeit sometimes unwittingly, a cadre of fundamental practices, which they referred to as their 4 + 2 formula.[8] The study singles out four primary management practices that were found to consistently drive corporate performance. They are:

1. Possess clear, focused, well-communicated strategy. (PRIDE Principles #s 1 and 4)

2. Displays superb operational execution. (PRIDE Principle #5)

3. Has a performance-oriented culture. (PRIDE Principle #2)

4. Possess a flat, flexible organizational structure. (PRIDE Principle #3)[9]

The study showcases Dell Computer as an exemplar of companies that closely follow these four principles. Dell has had an unswerving commitment to providing superior customer service. Dell's goals were well defined and communicated, and it relentlessly pursued flawless execution of its strategy. Dell has committed almost all its resources to its direct-distribution strategy (note: not budgets, *strategy*). Does it make a difference? Dell's profits have grown about 40 percent annually, while its competitors struggled to realize 2 percent growth.

GRAND STRATEGY ALIGNMENT MAPS

Painting the Strategic Landscape

A great method for applying the SBfV PRIDE principles, communicating the CEO's intent, and practicing operational art is to develop and employ strategy alignment maps, which are a logical, comprehensive, and visible architecture for describing and communicating strategic intent. These maps address the four questions that we expect a grand strategy to address:

1. What conditions (economic, political, diplomatic, operational, informational, and social) must be produced internally and externally to achieve the strategic goal(s)? (Ends)
2. What sequence of actions is most likely to produce that condition? (Ways)
3. How should resources, namely our Six Levels of Capital, be applied to accomplish that sequence of actions? (Means)
4. What is the risk or cost to the company in performing that sequence of actions, and, is it acceptable?

An alignment map presents the logical architecture that defines a company's strategy by specifying the relationship among shareholders or stakeholders, customer capital, systems capital, and the financial, human, organizational, and physical capital of assets and activities. It is a highly effective way for leaders to show how their goals would be accomplished by breaking their vision down into manageable pieces. Kaplan and Norton metaphorically refer to an organization's alignment map as the *recipe*.[10] The recipe is the corporate strategy that combines internal resources and capabilities to create unique value propositions for specific market segments and targeted customers within those identified segments. The recipe combines the tangible and intangible assets of the firm with existing and new capabilities that energize the value creation and conversion potential within the organization. Alignment maps provide the foundation for building a strategy implementation system that converts the new organizational potential into profit and enhanced market position. Alignment maps and SBfV's strategy execution model address the shortcomings of today's static financial measurement, management, and reporting systems. Strategy maps and SBfV's alignment and measurement process provide executives with an organic instrument to communicate how shareholder or stakeholder value is realized from different combinations of tangible and intangible assets in differing sequences. It forces one to develop the mindsets, models, and measures you need to lead in this knowledge-based world where intangibles rule in maximizing your value.

Crafting Strategy Alignment Maps

The formulation of strategy is an art. The communication of strategy is a responsibility. The execution of strategy is about practicing operational art. All of it is about leadership.

The SBfV Framework is a flexible tool for communicating leadership's intent. It is easily adapted into a specific alignment map for a company to cascade the leadership's strategic intent to the lowest business unit in the company (see Exhibit 3.1). It makes the strategy's embedded assumptions explicit to everyone. It is leadership's responsibility to continually challenge these assumptions for validity and reliability. A proven success factor in executing strategy is having everyone in the company clearly understand the underlying assumptions that support the strategy. To have everyone make their decisions based on the criteria "is it right for our ability to execute our strategy and make money?" To allocate, by choice, the resources they control or influence to those activities, projects, and tasks that have a direct or indirect effect in moving their piece of the company in

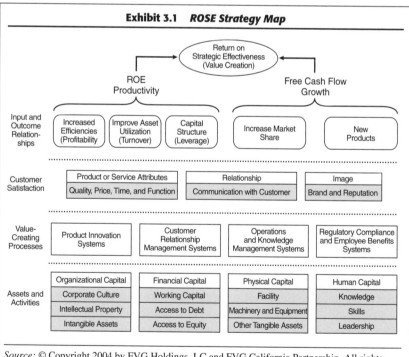

Exhibit 3.1 ROSE Strategy Map

Source: © Copyright 2004 by FVG Holdings, LC and FVG California Partnership. All rights reserved. Used with permission.

the direction of strategic intent. To have everyone continuously work to adapt to changes that affect strategic outcomes and to instill the institutional foresight to develop the knowledge and skill sets that the company will need to sustain those core competencies required to compete and make money in an uncertain future.

Exhibit 3.2 is an example of a strategy map adopted from the SBfV Framework and used to communicate a for-profit retail company's strategy to emphasize customer intimacy. Exhibit 3.3 is an example of a strategy map adopted from the SBfV Framework and used to communicate a not-for-profit public sector company's strategy of Operational Excellence. A strategy alignment map should clearly portray what the strategic intent is from the uppermost dimension of the company, whether this pertains to a for-profit or not-for-profit company. In Exhibit 3.2 (for-profit), the return on equity and free cash flow objectives frame strategic intent for the application of customer capital, systems capital, and assets and activities. In Exhibit 3.3 (not-for-profit), constituent objectives frame strategic intent for the financial (stakeholders), customers, internal business process, and employee and organizational capacity.

In crafting a strategy alignment map, the Financial and Customer Dimensions are the desired effects (strategic objectives) that always have lagging performance measures assigned. Sometimes, one or two leading performance measures, such as number of prospects contacted, are assigned to customer objectives for trend and regression analysis. The Systems or Processes and Human Capital Dimensions are the causes (strategic objectives) that usually have both lagging and leading performance measures assigned.

In SBfV strategy alignment maps, we recognize four tiers of value dimensions: (1) Input and Outcome Relationships, (2) Customer Satisfaction, (3) The Value-Creating Process, and (4) Integration of Assets and Activities. Strategic intent is driven from top to bottom in the map; value creation is driven from bottom to top.

Cause-and-effect linkages should be transparent between the tiered dimensions' objectives. We operationally define the four dimensional tiers based on the company's outcome of objectives or effects desired by presenting the following:

1. **Input and Outcome Relationships**—Demonstrates the chain of logic by which the tangible and intangible assets will be converted into value for the stakeholders/stockholders. (Ends)

2. **Customer Satisfaction**— Identifies the conditions that satisfy the customers and therefore allows the company to achieve its financial return as strategy. (Ways)

3. **Value Creating Processes**—Defines the critical systems that will transform the assets and activities in customer and financial outcomes. (Means)

Exhibit 3.2 Retail (For Profit) Company's "ROSE" Map (Customer Intimacy)

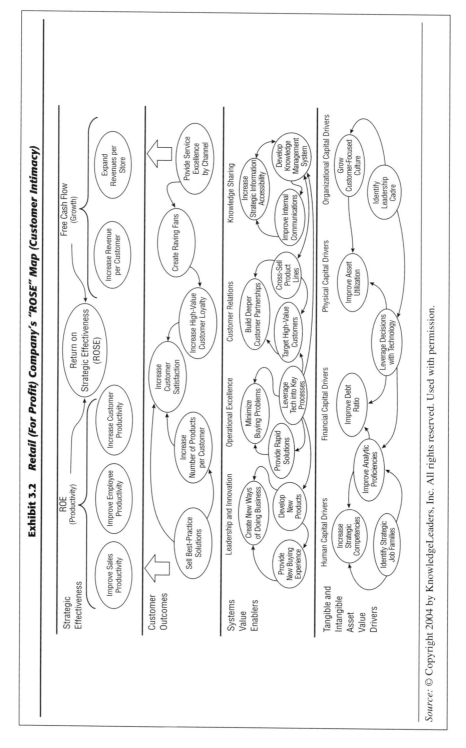

Exhibit 3.3 Public Sector (Not-for-Profit) Company's "ROSE" Map (Operational Excellence)

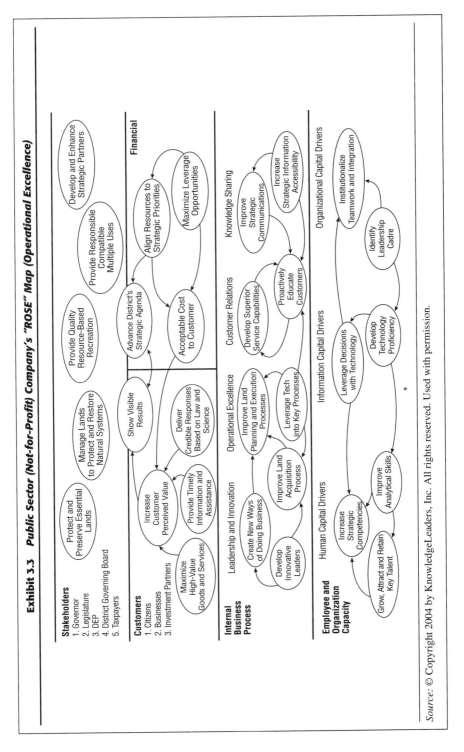

Stakeholders
1. Governor
2. Legislature
3. DEP
4. District Governing Board
5. Taxpayers

Customers
1. Citizens
2. Businesses
3. Investment Partners

Internal Business Process

Employee and Organization Capacity

4. Integration of Assets and Activities—Defines the tangible and intangible assets that must be integrated to increase the company's value. (Means)

Holding strategic themes consistent throughout the dimensions of the Six Levels of Capital is the core of leadership. Strategic themes can be used to organize all the objectives that will ultimately make up the company's strategy map. Strategic themes help mobilize and bring market relevance to strategic intent. These themes are developed around value propositions (Operational Excellence, Customer Intimacy, and Product Leadership) and serve to link strategic objectives between the tiered dimensions. Each theme should have a clear effect on the end-state dimension (i.e., For-profits: Financial; Not-for-Profits: Constituents or Stakeholders).

Guided by strategic themes, strategic objectives are the action statements within each dimension that clarify how the company will execute the strategy. They are the linked set of priorities in cause-and-effect sequencing that will most likely deliver the strategy. They clarify the ends, ways, and means of the strategy. Strategic objectives should:

1. Contextually fit in the cause-and-effect chain.
2. Add value in telling the strategy story.
3. Reflect logical and systems thinking.
4. Be actionable (Verb + Descriptor + Result).
5. Be measurable.

Examples of strategic objectives statements generated from strategy maps are presented in Exhibit 3.4, "City of Charlotte Corporate Strategy Map" and Exhibit 3.5, "District/IRD Strategy Alignment Business Model."

The SBfV organizational alignment process begins, for most for-profit companies, with a top-down cascade with strategic themes set in the context of the ROE components of free cash flow and return on equity outcomes.

Increasing a company's ROE requires that managers make all strategic decisions focusing on one of the *Five Dimensions of Value*. Every strategic action in order to create value must correspond to one or more of these Five Dimensions of Value. The Five Dimensions of Value are all related to growth and productivity within the company:

1. Increase market share using a constant capital investment. (Growth Dimension)
2. Invest capital in projects that yield a higher economic return, such as a new product line. (Growth Dimension)

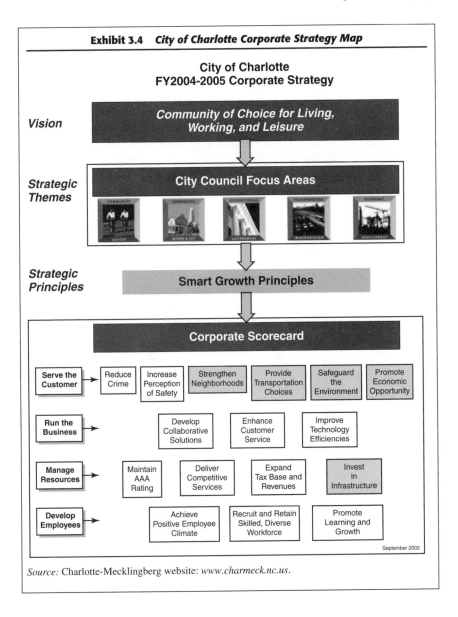

Exhibit 3.4 *City of Charlotte Corporate Strategy Map*

City of Charlotte
FY2004-2005 Corporate Strategy

Source: Charlotte-Mecklingberg website: *www.charmeck.nc.us.*

Exhibit 3.5 District/RD Strategy Alignment Business Model

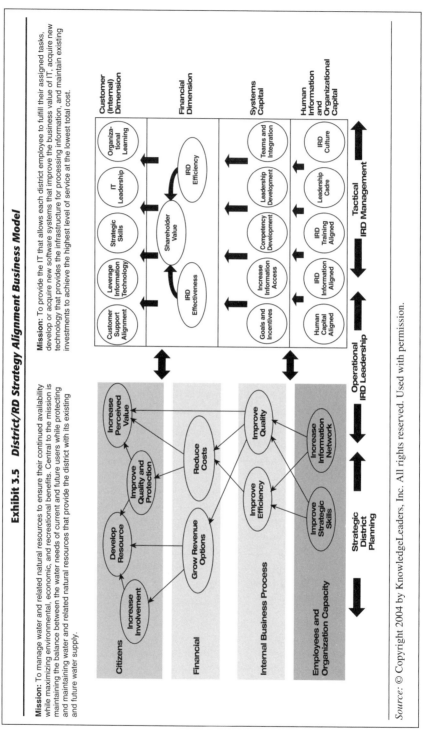

Mission: To manage water and related natural resources to ensure their continued availability while maximizing environmental, economic, and recreational benefits. Central to the mission is maintaining the balance between the water needs of current and future users while protecting and maintaining water and related natural resources that provide the district with its existing and future water supply.

Mission: To provide the IT that allows each district employee to fulfill their assigned tasks, develop or acquire new software systems that improve the business value of IT, acquire new technology that provides the infrastructure for processing information, and maintain existing investments to achieve the highest level of service at the lowest total cost.

3. Increase profit through operating efficiencies while using a constant capital structure. (Productivity Dimension)

4. Maintain profit while using less capital through improved asset turnover. (Productivity Dimension)

5. Maintain or improve profit, while lowering the weighted average cost of capital (WACC). (Productivity Dimension)

Management must focus their management decision making on strategic initiatives that are analyzed against the Five Dimensions of Value. Every decision should question if the action will accomplish the goals of one or more of the dimensions of value.

The first of the five dimensions, increase market share using a constant capital investment, is based on the fact that long-term consistent growth in profits can only be accomplished by expanding the company's market share and therefore its growth in gross revenues.

Temporarily the growth in the size of the marketplace may increase revenues without a larger market share, but eventually most markets flatten or decline in size due to many factors such as new technology or changes in consumers buying habits. Management must continually focus its marketing efforts on increasing its market share.

The second of the five dimensions, invest capital in projects that yield a higher economic return, such as a new product line, is based on the simple fact that a higher profit margin will increase the company's free cash flow. An investment in a new higher-margin product line will increase cash flows in two ways. First, each dollar of sales will provide more free cash flow than the older product line. Second, new products will produce additional revenue from an expanded product line.

The third dimension of value, increase profit through operating efficiencies while using a constant capital structure, recognizes the fact that profits and the related free cash flow can be increased by implementing operating efficiencies that lower operating costs without requiring any investments in new assets. For example, companies can use overtime or a second shift without significant capital expenditures as opposed to building a new factory or a factory addition.

The fourth dimension, maintain profit while using less capital through improved asset turnover, is based on the concept that excess assets or excess assets created from increased efficiencies will lower capital invested in the company, if these excess assets are distributed to the stockholders. Alternately, this additional free cash flow from liquidating the excess assets can then be invested in other activities, which will increase the shareholders' total personal returns and total personal net worth without decreasing the value of the company.

The fifth dimension, maintain or improve profit while lowering the weighted average cost of capital (WACC), recognizes that a company may not be using its available debt appropriately. Many companies are utilizing very little debt, which raises their cost of capital and lowers these companies' value. Utilizing appropriate debt levels works in conjunction with the fourth dimension to create free cash flows, which can be distributed to the stockholders or used to reduce the need for additional cash investments from the stockholders.

Management decisions that utilize the Five Dimensions of Value will cause the company to develop a management style that focuses on value creation.

With the financial strategic objectives specified, the cascade continues down to the customer dimension for presenting a unique value proposition to the market. What combinations of customer profiles and unique product and service mix will generate greater economic profits? The value proposition should define how your company uniquely differentiates itself in this market segment to retain high-value customers, attract new customers, and increase net revenues from existing customers.

Continuing the cascade, strategy's value enablers and value drivers really exist in the Systems and Human Capital Dimensions of the alignment map. The Systems Dimension focuses on the key structured capabilities, purposeful patterns of interaction, and core processes with associated support tasks and activities that you will need to excel at to meet or exceed customer expectations for that unique value proposition defined in the Customer Dimension. This is where intrinsic value is converted to explicit value in some form of a value exchange.

Last, the Human Capital Dimension conveys the deep appreciation that in order to excel in the processes that will deliver that unique value proposition, human capital will need to have distinct skills, possess certain knowledge, and build specific core competencies. Moreover, SBfV's Alignment Model will proactively build in a measurable degree of absorptive capacity that will give your company the capability to drive new knowledge vertically and horizontally across the company's entire value network.

A company's grand strategy alignment map provides the context and a powerful framework for lower-level divisions, departments, business units, work teams, and individuals to describe, prioritize, resource, and implement their lower-level strategies and tactics. Most companies consist of many different service or business units (SBUs) as well as shared service or supporting units. For maximum value growth, the strategies, tactics, and resource allocation should be aligned and linked together. The alignment and linkages across different strategy map levels mobilize the concept of managing decentralized business units and shared service units under a single strategy umbrella. These strategic linkages make up the strategic architecture of the company. That is, the ends, ways, and means to create added value through synergy by integrating and synchronizing the disparate activities of functionally segregated units. We view this as the purpose of the corporate entity—to create synergies among the business and service support units. For example, financial organizations such as Bank of America (BofA) have strategies that involve providing a broad set of financial services such as credit cards, mortgages, loans, and checking services to the same customers. Each of these services is delivered by a different SBU that historically operates independently from other service providers. The role of the corporation is to create synergy through the sharing of customers across SBUs. Through strategic intent communicated in their strategy alignment map, the corporate strategy then should emphasize such objectives as: the sharing of resources and expenses, cross-selling, and integrated products. Leadership should then further translate corporate intent into a set of strategic priorities through effects-based strategy trees, prioritization tools, apportionment of effort guidance, resource to strategy allocation determinations, and performance measures.

ALIGNMENT THESIS AND VALUE PROPOSITIONS

In the SBfV Alignment Model, the free cash flow outcomes within the return on strategic effectiveness framework provide the context (strategic intent) to frame the strategic thesis that runs throughout the alignment map and value network tree. For example, with a growth outcome objective (G1) to increase market share by 10 percent using constant capital, then one of your strategic thesis may be to "increase customer perceived value." In general, strategic theses reflect leaderships' assumption of what must be done internally to achieve that growth strategic outcome. A *thesis* is the "river" that runs through a strategy's dimensions and should be closely aligned with the "value proposition" delivered to the customer. The value proposition describes the unique mix of product or service attributes, customer relationships, and company image that you are offering targeted customers. The center of gravity of any business strategy is the value proposition delivered to the customer. The succinct value proposition provides the focus for the development of the strategic thesis.

As we discussed in Step 1, there are three different strategies any company adopts to differentiate itself in the marketplace.[11] They are:

1. **Cost Efficient or Operational Excellence**—Companies pursuing this differentiation deliver high-quality products and services with great accessibility for a price that others cannot match. This requires high-quality and cost-efficient operating processes, strong supplier relations, and highly efficient distribution processes (as exemplified by Southwest Airlines, Dell Computer).

2. **Product Innovation**—Companies pursuing this differentiation provide the latest state-of-the-art product attributes. They are torchbearers in product development. This requires leading-edge innovation processes and support systems that create new products with best-in-class functionality and speed-to-market capability (as exemplified by Intel, Microsoft, DOW Chemical).

3. **Customer Intimacy**—Companies pursuing this differentiation build strong relationships with their customers. They know their customer's buying patterns and can anticipate their product and service needs. This requires excellent customer management processes and customer relationship support systems (as exemplified by The Home Depot, Wal-Mart, Lexus, etc.).

Treacy and Wiersema argue that successful companies work hard to excel at one of these three value propositions and maintain "threshold standards" in the other two.[12] For example, companies pursuing a Customer Intimacy strategy like The Home Depot stress the quality of their relationships with customers and the comprehensive solution sets it can provide vis-à-vis competitors. Companies pursuing an Operational Excellence strategy need to excel in quality, price, delivery, and service, and do it better than their competition in that market. Companies pursuing a product and service leadership strategy need to excel in uniqueness, product features and unequaled performance of their product or service.

The choice of which value proposition to brand affects the targeted customer base selection. Which group of potential customers value customer intimacy in their buying experience with providers? Which market segment values the latest innovations or values products that endure because of their outstanding manufacturing quality? So, as you select which value proposition to market you are also selecting what customer base to pursue based on those customers' values.

Purpose Drives the Strategy Execution Value Continuum

The customer value proposition and how you transform it into growth and profitability for investors is the heart of strategy execution. These realized outcomes are the result of strategy. But how you optimally combine all your efforts and resources to achieve these outcomes is the differentiator for successful leaders regardless of your company's business. Here, Porter argues that, "The essence of strategy is in the activities—choosing to perform activities differently or performing different activities than rivals."[13] We argue that activities will give your company a competitive advantage *only* if those activities are aligned and aimed at realizing the customer value proposition identified in your strategy. Then, that

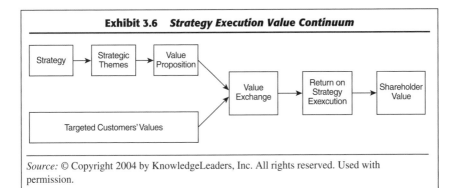

Exhibit 3.6   *Strategy Execution Value Continuum*

proposition will only carry value if it is targeted against the right customer segment whose values "value" the offer. This is demonstrated in Exhibit 3.6. Intuitively obvious to many, well practiced by only the best.

The activities of a company come to life with the interactions of people and systems. These interactions usually happen within the functional realms of: operations, management, marketing, and finance administration. Within these functional areas people and processes iteratively develop competencies. These competencies are important and must be performed well to survive as a company. But companies must develop a core competency that has maximum impact on delivering the customer value proposition to the targeted market segment in order to sustain competitive advantage. What core competency is needed for a company that adopts an Operational Excellence strategy in order to deliver perceived and valued quality attributes for unmatched prices to the market as its value proposition? What core competency is needed for a company that adopts a Product Leadership strategy in order to deliver unique products and services that are "leading edge" in the market as its value proposition? What core competency is needed for a company that adopts a Customer Intimacy strategy in order to deliver personalized and tailored services with a trusted brand to the market as its value proposition?

ACHIEVING STRATEGIC ALIGNMENT

What Strategy Alignment Is Not

An SBfV strategic alignment is not simply about being operationally efficient, nor is strategy execution simply more talk about operational effectiveness. Strategic alignment goes beyond the usual cost- and efficiency-based comparisons and looks instead at ways of measuring the alignment of systems investment and human capital employment with business strategy. Operational efficiency and operational effectiveness are necessary, but not sufficient. SBfV alignments are much more. They incorporate efficient and effectiveness in support of strategy to achieve operational excellence in the marketplace. Strategy execution is about synchronizing ways, means, and ends to efficiently and effectively sustain building value through measured growth and productivity outcomes.

It is not simply a compendium of your business unit operational plans compiled into a huge binder and reviewed every six months. It is not a list of all the projects and initiatives your company is conducting or plans to conduct. It is not about formulating mission, vision, and values. It is not just about project management. It is not about establishing policies and corporate governance. It is not about compensation and rewards. It is not about networked and integrated computers. It is not about accounting and budgets. It is not about compliance and regulatory practices. It is a not an action plan. It is not just about knowledge management. It is not just about leadership development and succession planning. It is not just about risk management. It is not about activity-based costing. It is not just about performance measurements. It is not about EVA, REVA, or EBITDA. It appears it is NOT about a lot . . . but, it is a lot.

SBfV strategy alignments specify how all the moving parts of a company will be synchronized to achieve targeted objectives. SBfV ties the thread through the three core factors for executing strategy: the strategy itself, the people who have to implement the strategy, and all the supporting systems that enable and empower the people to execute the strategy.

Alignment or "strategy fit" provides synchronization within companies. Synchronization means that all the moving parts of a company have common assumptions about the internal and external environment and a common understanding of purpose and direction—the left hand knows what the right hand is doing. Synchronization entails matching the goals and mental models of the interdependent parts and linking their priorities with the other parts of the company. When situations change, a synchronized company rapidly reprioritizes objectives, realigns the apportionment of effort, and reallocates resources.

$$(\text{Strategy}) \times (\text{Systems}) \times (\text{People}) \times (\text{Synchronization}) = \text{Synergy}$$
$$\text{Synergy} = \text{Value (Economic Profits)}$$

Strategy Alignment's Critical Role in Maximizing Value

In today's knowledge-based economy, senior executives are faced with the challenge of optimizing their investment in systems capital and human capital to help their business:

- Execute strategy.
- Improve productivity.
- Enhance the perceived value of its own products and services.

To capture the full value of a company, it is essential to closely align strategic and operational planning. Our SBfV Alignment Model does just that. The model focuses on three key elements—strategy, systems, and people—that need to be managed synchronously or aligned to derive full value from all three factors. It provides a systematic way of planning a successful business strategy with the necessary systems and people infrastructure to support it. It provides a practical and powerful way to ensure that businesses get the full benefit from their investment in systems and people. It is a means of giving order with clarity to the process of bringing a company's business plan and budget into harmony with the infrastructure to make the plan work. Only when the business strategy, the systems, and the people have been aligned can the business advance successfully.

Companies seem to find it difficult or impossible to harness the synergy of people and systems for their long-term benefit. The problem is that too much attention is placed on systems or people independent of their links and leverage effects on other business operations, customer value propositions, and each other. They fail to recognize the importance of building organizational structures, sets of business processes, and product and service offerings that reflect the interdependence of enterprise strategy, system's capabilities, and people's skill sets that yield the core competencies to sustain long-term growth and productivity.

Our SBfV strategy alignment is a powerful, but simple model. It recognizes that different people in a company make, at different times, different sets of business decisions. The alignment process emphasizes that the decisions need to be coordinated to achieve maximum value.

As shown in Exhibit 3.7, decisions on business strategy set the direction of the enterprise based on an understanding of the enterprise's resources, capabilities, and competencies; the competition's resources, capabilities, and competencies; market needs; and strategic postures. These strategy decisions provide structure for available resources to best compete. Decisions about business support infrastructure are often designed in considerable detail after the strategy decisions are made. However, from our experience, we submit that infrastructure design must be coupled to: the projected operational environment, the enterprise-wide strategy, the systems capability, and peoples' competencies. Managing infrastructure is often a matter of making careful decisions on what capability you really need to own, and when, to support the business strategy.

Exhibit 3.7 Strategy Decision Cell

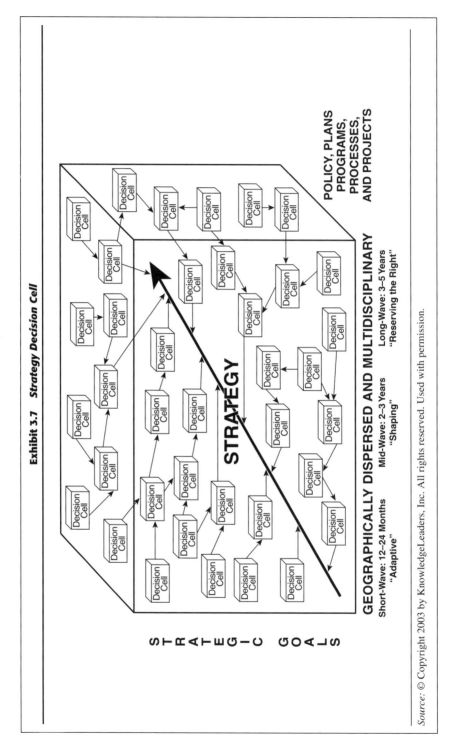

Decisions on systems and people strategy, intended to translate business strategy into a competent infrastructure that allows the enterprise to compete effectively, are often made after the decisions on business strategy. These complementary strategy decisions must also influence the initial decision on business strategy, since not all things are possible in either the people or systems strategies independent of the business strategy itself. These three sets of decisions—on business strategy, systems strategy, and people strategy—need to be closely coordinated, or what we call "aligned." The problem for companies striving for alignment is far greater than just overcoming technical systems' incompatibility. The relationship of these three factors of alignment will be expounded on more deeply later in the chapter.

One of the basic research questions is whether attention paid to the dimensions and relationships that define strategic alignment influences organizational action toward the marketplace. Indeed, study results indicate that when top managers have a heightened understanding of the relationship between business strategy and systems strategy (strategic linkage), it is likely that they are better equipped to identify how systems can promote or facilitate changes in the scope of the business. Specifically, the findings showed that understanding the implications of strategic linkage led to the adoption of more innovative hospital products and services over the subsequent two-year period. Such products and services adopted or implemented included open-heart surgical facilities, organ or tissue transplants, burn care units, neonatal intensive care units, and diagnostic radioisotope facilities.

In contrast, when managers focused their attention on, and showed a greater understanding of, the relationship between organizational infrastructure and systems infrastructure (functional linkage), they were less likely to initiate innovative changes in their hospitals' product and service portfolios. That is, they reduced, or did not significantly add to, their product and service portfolio (added services that were not considered innovative—e.g., respiratory therapy, hemodialysis). Clearly, these managers were attempting to identify how systems and organizational structures could be modified to improve implementation of the existing product and service line or, if expansion did occur, that it was for the purpose of including more "basic" services in the portfolio.

Findings also suggest that innovative changes in the product and service offerings can potentially impact multiple dimensions of organizational performance. For example, the addition of innovative customer services (such as cardiac catheterization in the hospital setting) increased the ability of the company to serve a diverse group of customers and clients, thereby increasing the scope and overall effectiveness of the company. Conversely, simply maintaining existing services and focusing primarily on the efficiency of their delivery might result in stagnation of the customer base and revenues.

A focus on strategic linkage is associated with increased innovativeness, while having a top-management team that focuses on functional linkage is associated with decreased or stagnating innovativeness. The final skill set needed to convert strategic linkage to profit was a deep understanding of the implications and importance of business fit (i.e., the relationship between a business strategy and the organizational systems and people).

In summary, as the preceding review of the concept-testing studies done in strategic alignment suggests, strategic alignment is a potentially powerful explanation and predictor of successful organizational transformation.

How can valid measures be developed that allow for the accurate assessment of a company's strategic alignment? In what manner does alignment evolve over time? Are certain patterns or perspectives more prevalent or successful than others? Under what conditions are they?

As studies begin to provide prescriptive and normative insights to top managers regarding the planning for, and implementation of, strategic alignment, we need to formulate answers to these critical questions. This requires that we support and refine the conceptual and exploratory developments that have dominated the study of strategic alignment through empirical testing coupled with sound—and even creative—assessment tools and methods.

Ultimately, the goal should be to identify how alignment is manifested in the behaviors and systems of the company.

A STRATEGY ALIGNMENT MODEL THAT WORKS—SBfV

The SBfV Alignment Model

The Strategic Benchmarking for Value (SBfV) Alignment Model (Exhibit 3.8) is a step-by-step method to engineer improved value. SBfV's improved efficiencies and effectiveness are equally applicable to for-profit and not-for-profit companies.

The SBfV Alignment Model aligns a company's purpose and strategy with its systems and people. Alignment is not just a buzzword. For companies that are really serious about peak performance, it is a strategic imperative. For those companies that adhere to its guidance, alignment provides the sequence of events and strategic benchmarks needed to realize maximum value.

The SBfV Alignment Model connects the dots between value and strategy execution, producing maximum economic profits through optimal growth and pro-

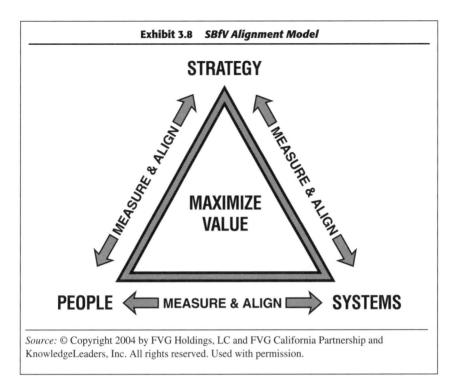

Exhibit 3.8 SBfV Alignment Model

STRATEGY

MEASURE & ALIGN

MEASURE & ALIGN

MAXIMIZE
VALUE

PEOPLE ⟵ MEASURE & ALIGN ⟶ SYSTEMS

ductivity. The SBfV Alignment Model gives your company the ability to apply the lessons of modern warfare to execute your business strategy. The SBfV Alignment Model is an adaptation of the military's strategy execution model so successfully displayed in Iraqi Freedom. Today, we believe that the only sustainable source of competitive advantage any company has is its ability to execute strategy faster and more effectively than its competition.

The heart of maximizing the value of any company is how the three factors of strategy, systems, and people align and link together. Nothing is more important to maximize the value of any company than developing leaders who know how to synchronize these three core factors. The biggest single difference between businesses that successfully execute their strategy and those that do not is the rigor and intensity with which the leader prosecutes these factors.

The SBfV Alignment Model provides management with measured results in performance against strategy-driven outcomes. SBfV alignments will help you answer such pressing questions as:

1. What is a reliable way to monitor the value of my company?
2. What are the dimensions of value specific to my company?
3. What are the real value drivers of my company?
4. How can management identify the critical decisions that would most affect growth, productivity, and value?
5. How can management execute decisions to grow, which specifically improve economic profits?
6. How can management verify that their growth and productivity decisions are really working?
7. Of the total population of financial and nonfinancial performance measures, which ones most affect value? That is, where is the biggest bang for the buck?
8. How can I use the "shock and awe" resource apportionment and allocation logic applied in Iraqi Freedom to achieve the highest value for my company?
9. What intellectual capital within the Six Levels of Capital most affects value?
10. Which business processes (management, marketing, finance and administration, operations) most affect value?
11. What is my real cost of invested capital and economic profits?
12. How can I best balance revenue growth strategies and cost-cutting productivity strategies?
13. How can I best align short- and long-term goals, strategies, and scarce resources?
14. Are my value-growth decisions being executed through all reporting units?

On Systems: Linking Strategy with People

Today, when we use the word "systems" most people conjure up mental models of: computers, software, applications, IT, MIS, ERP, SAP, CRM, and so forth. They would be correct, but they would also be suboptimizing complexity. These technology-related systems are really subsystems of a greater enterprise system that is better captured by our previous discussion on systems capital, but be careful what you synergize. The rule of It All Depends (IAD) applies here. Applying IAD reflects context-based strategy execution and is not just a cop-out for tough questions. IAD on how tightly your company's systems and people are aligned with your strategy. You may have multimillion-dollar systems multiplying the wrong things. So, not only do you have to deal with procurement, operational, maintenance, and upgrading IT costs, you need to factor in the potential losses of misalignment. All companies must be viewed as a system, and the work people do within the systems must be seen as processes. Deming and others suggest that more than 85 percent of all things that go wrong in any organization are directly attributable to how the organization's system and processes are set up and perpetuate the patterns of interaction.[14]

Systems thinkers pay attention to the ways that people and things interconnect and work to understand the many levels on which these relationships are built.

> A cloud masses, the sky darkens, leaves twist upward, and we know that it will rain. We also know that after the storm, the runoff will feed into groundwater miles away, and the sky will grow clear by tomorrow. All these events are distant in time and space, and yet they are all connected within the same pattern. Each has an influence on the rest, an influence that is usually hidden from view. You can only understand the system of rainstorm by contemplating the whole, not any individual part of the pattern.[15]

Systems thinking is a conceptual framework, a body of knowledge with sophisticated tools that have been developed over the past 60 years to make full patterns of interaction clearer and more manageable and, in doing so, make them more predictable. When mastering the dynamic complexity essential to successful strategy, it is easy to get lost in the trees and lose sight of the forest. Here is where SBfV's discipline of systems thinking imparts great competitive advantage through continuous adaptation. By using our SBfV Alignment Model you can learn how to "structure" the details into a coherent picture of the forces at play in executing your strategy. SBfV incorporates systems thinking as an organizational learning alternative to the pervasive "reductionism" in our Western culture—the pursuit of simple answers to complex issues.

In today's knowledge-based world, uncertainty abounds and market forces are constantly changing. The fundamental assumptions and core theory of "market equilibrium," while mathematically elegant, are static. Using a traditional approach to strategy encompassing market forces may lead executives to underestimate uncertainty.

Today's executives must realize that in most cases they are trying to guide and direct complex adaptive systems (CASs) and not the closed equilibrium systems of the past that shaped their current mental models. CASs share the following three characteristics. First, they are open, dynamic systems of perpetual motion where patterns of behavior are constantly shifting; some patterns appear stable others chaotic. Second, these systems are made up of interacting components, such as people or computers. What each component does affects one or more of the other components at least some of the time; this makes outcomes difficult to predict. Third, CASs exhibit emergence and self-organization. Individual ants do not do much, but put them in a group where they can interact, and an anthill emerges. Because the anthill emerges out of the bottom-up dynamic interactions of the ants and not from a top-down master blueprint, it is characterized as self-organized.

How do systems (complex and adaptive) link people to strategy? When placed in the same system, people, however different, tend to produce similar results. Just like the dynamic interaction of ants creates an anthill structure, the dynamic interaction of people within systems creates "systemic structures" in companies. The SBfV Alignment Model provides a truly profound and different insight in the way you begin to see that "systemic structures" cause its own behavior. The SBfV process identifies your systemic structures that are concerned with the key interrelationships that influence behavior over time. These are not just interrelationships between people but among all key organizational components—tangible and intangible. Systemic structures can drive, support, or restrain your strategy and desired changes. They generate the patterns of behavior that run your company. Understanding your structural systems' alignment is critical because only with that understanding can you address the underlying causes of organizational behavior at a level that allows patterns of behavior to be changed. Structure produces behavior, and realigning underlying structures can produce different patterns of behavior.

SBfV provides the structure for CASs to align patterns of behavior with strategy. An SBfV system's alignment includes all the activities, initiatives, programs, policies, plans, and projects that improve operational efficiencies. SBfV specifies how all the moving parts of an organization will be synchronized to achieve targeted objectives. SBfV ties the thread through the three core factors for executing strategy: the strategy itself, the people who have to implement the strategy, and all the supporting systems that enable and empower the people to execute the strategy.

When systems are properly aligned with people and strategy they add measurable value. When systems are not aligned with people and strategy they destroy value. Alignment or "systems fit" provides synchronization within companies. Synchronization means that all the moving parts of a company have common assumptions about the internal and external environment and a common understanding of purpose and direction—the left hand knows what the right hand is doing. Synchronization entails matching the goals and mental models of the interdependent parts and linking their priorities with the other parts of the company.

When situations change, a synchronized company rapidly reprioritizes objectives, realigns the apportionment of effort, and reallocates resources.

NOTES

1. David P. Norton, *Balanced Scorecard Report*, Vol. 3, No. 5, (September/October 2001), Reprint #B0109A.
2. Gary Hamel and C.K Prahalad, "Strategy as Stretch and Leverage," reprinted in Susan Segal-Horn, *The Strategy Reader* (Blackwell Publishers, 1998), p. 49.
3. Robert S. Kaplan and David P. Norton, *The Strategy-Focused Organization* (Boston: Harvard Business School Press, 2001), p. 1.
4. Stephen R. Covey, *Principle-Centered Leadership* (New York: Fireside, 1991), p. 68.
5. *Ibid.*, p. 69.
6. *Ibid.*, p. 19.
7. Peter Jacobs, *Why Most Management Tools Don't Work* (Boston: Harvard Business School Publishing, 2003), p. 3.
8. *Ibid.* p. 3
9. *Ibid.* p. 4
10. Robert S. Kaplan and David P. Norton, *The Strategy-Focused Organization* (Boston: Harvard Business School Press, 2001), pp. 10–11.
11. M. Treacy and F. Wiersema, *The Discipline of Market Leaders: Choose Your Customers, Narrow Your Focus, Dominate Your Market* (Reading, MA: Addison-Wesley, 1995).
12. *Ibid.*
13. Michael Porter, "What Is Strategy?" *Harvard Business Review* (November/December, 1996), p. 62
14. W. Edwards Deming, *Out of Crisis* (Cambridge: MA: MIT Press, 2000).
15. Peter M. Senge, *The Fifth Discipline* (Currency Doubleday, 1990), pp. 6–7.

STEP 4

Alignment Execution

ALIGNMENT EXECUTION

This chapter is about putting it together. It is the alignment of the strategy, systems, and people that make the SBfV Process work. In a word, it is about "execution." As John McCay, the original coach of the Tampa Bay Buccaneers football team, once said after a poor performance:

Reporter: "Coach, what do you think about your team's execution?"

McCay: "I'm in favor of it."[1]

A study of 275 portfolio managers reported that the ability to execute strategy was more important than the quality of the strategy itself.[2] These managers cited strategy implementation as the most important factor shaping management and corporate valuations. In a 1999 *Fortune* article on some prominent CEO failures, the authors concluded that the heavy emphasis placed on vision and strategy created an incorrect assurance that having the right strategy was the panacea for success. Charan and Colvin found that in about 70 percent of the failures the real problem was not bad strategy, but rather "bad execution."[3]

Why is there such difficulty in implementing well-formulated strategies? Possibly Clausewitz best captured the essence of the leadership challenge in 1832 when he said, "Everything in strategy is very simple, but that does not mean that everything is very easy. Once it has been determined, from the political conditions, what a war is meant to achieve and what it can achieve, it is easy to chart the course. But great strength of character, as well as great lucidity and firmness of mind, is required in order to follow through steadily, to carry out the plan, and not be thrown off course by thousands of diversions."[3] On your financial reports, how do you measure, manage, and record the intangible contributions of character, lucidity, and firmness of mind?

Clearly, opportunities for creating value have shifted from managing the tangibles to managing knowledge-based intangibles. In today's economy, and as far as we can see into the future, intellectual capital is the major source of competitive advantage. This knowledge-based economy calls for tools that: better describe intellectual capital, measure its relationship to tangible outcomes, identify efficient cause-and-effect sequencing, and manage the value-creating strategies that these assets of uncertainty make possible. Lacking these systems and tools, companies will continue to experience significant difficulty extracting full value from their intangible assets. Thus forecasting models that drive resource allocation decisions will remain impaired, and our national accounts will still be short by over $1 trillion (and growing).[4] We cannot manage intangibles with systems designed to measure and manage tangibles, and we cannot manage strategy with systems designed for tactics.

PUTTING IT TOGETHER

The designation of individual dimensions of the three dimensions of the SBfV Alignment Model, as well as the selection of one or more of the strategies (Operational Excellence, Product Leadership, Customer Intimacy), is only part of the overall leadership challenge to realize maximum value from invested capital. The SBfV Alignment Process creates the dynamic capabilities and core competencies to effectively transform any organization into a strategy execution-focused culture. Employing this approach and the SBfV Alignment Model requires an understanding of its inherent dynamic nature. Many of the strategic-planning methods popular in the 1970s and 1980s lost executive favor, not because of the weakness in their reasoning but because of their failure to adequately address the dynamic nature of strategy formulation and execution. Executives are painfully cognizant that the real business challenge is not static alignment among the three dimensions—strategy, systems, and people—at any given point in time. The real leadership challenge is how to ensure continual assessment of the movement across and between the three dimensions to allow strategic repositioning of the organization in the external market and the adept realignment of the internal infrastructure.

Focusing Accountability by Applying the SBfV Alignment Model

This section describes the measures and strategic planning method appropriate to four alignment perspectives of the SBfV Alignment Model, important enablers and hindrances of strategic alignment. It describes how organizations cycle through each perspective, starting by identifying which dimension offers the largest opportunity for improvement (the *fulcrum dimension*). Next the dimension providing the changes that will drive the fulcrum dimension is identified, and last, the dimension that will be affected by the improvements. This establishes the direction to transition around the SBfV triangle. Transitioning around the SBfV Alignment Model will only be effective if the strategy leadership team is clear about the organization's current and future objectives. The model forces challenging many assumptions about the business and can only be useful if the leadership team is prepared to address these with an open dialogue.

Understanding Alignment Dimensions

The strategic alignment model's components and the original four alignment perspectives were introduced in Step 3. We indicated that each was "driven" by a particular management orientation. Exhibit 4.1 illustrates one way of understanding these relationships.

Driver Dimension

In all cases, alignment starts out with the *driver dimension* within each perspective (as shown in Exhibit 4.1), which is the core enabler of the perspective—the driver of change. The driver dimension is the starting point. It is the dimension that is typically the most stable for the company. It is often the area in a business that has received most leadership attention. It is in a strong position to drive the strategy execution process.

Alignment Fulcrum Dimension

The *fulcrum dimension* is the area that offers the most potential for improvement. It holds the best opportunity to act as *force multiplier* in aligning the business. It also has great leverage potential. The *driver dimension* is the force to help move the fulcrum into a position of strength within the company.

Alignment Influenced Dimension

The last area, the *influenced dimension*, is the dimension that is being affected by the changes to the strategy execution fulcrum. Here, there is a real need for leadership to study and comprehend the implications of the anticipated changes to the impact area.

Enablers and Inhibitors of Strategic Alignment

In a strategic alignment assessment conducted by Luftman and Brier,[5] the first question asked participating executives to rate the strength of the alignment within their companies. Only half indicated that their firms were properly aligned. Over 42 percent indicated that their strategies were not aligned. Seven percent were unsure or had no opinion. The executives were then asked to rank the top enablers and inhibitors of achieving alignment. Executives agreed on the relative positioning of these enablers to alignment. They also agreed that within the top grouping, all enablers involved leadership and strategy development issues. Identifying these enablers is consequential, because they show how critical the involvement and support from top leadership is for achieving strategic alignment goals.

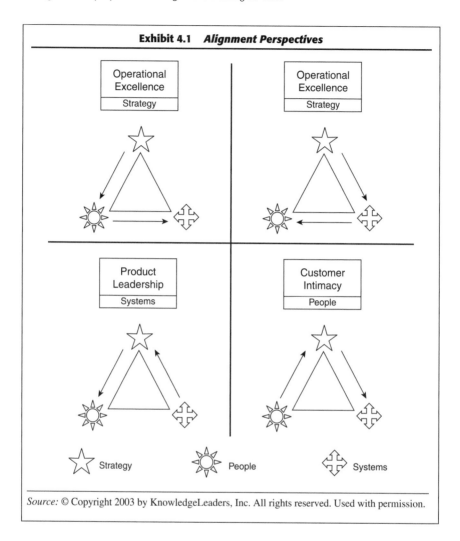

Exhibit 4.1 *Alignment Perspectives*

The assessment also revealed that the most common inhibitors of achieving alignment fell into the area of interdependence and synchronization. Business strategy, systems, operations, and people were going in different directions with poor communications and interactions between the alignment components. Executives believed that the greatest problem in achieving alignment was the lack of close relationship between strategists, system capital managers, and human capital developers. As a spillover cost from these distant relationships, the top inhibitor was identified to be poor prioritization across the company.

Application of the SBfV Alignment Model begins by identifying and assigning a cross-functional team from the major business units. Their knowledge of the business is key. The process begins by analyzing the current ("Where are we now?") and future ("Where should we go?") conditions for each of the alignment perspectives of the SBfV Alignment Model. The individual team members' perspectives and candid dialogue provide the initial activities that generate a contextually correct and current picture of the company's strengths, weaknesses, opportunities, and threats from which current and future analysis will provide the:

- Strategic intent, strategy thesis, and value proposition.
- New strategic objectives.
- New cause and effect linkages to achieve those objectives.
- Prioritized list of new opportunities available by leveraging core competencies through economic alignment.
- An apportionment of effort guide from top leadership.
- An instrument to articulate strategy throughout the organization.
- An instrument to prioritize systems and human capital investments.
- An instrument to allocate resources to projects and initiatives with strategic impact.

Perspectives and Dimensions Combination Flow Analysis

Operational Excellence: Strategy to People to Systems

This combination and sequence uses strategy as the driver dimension, people infrastructure as the fulcrum dimension, and systems infrastructure as the influenced dimension (see Exhibit 4.2). This combination and flow probably represent where most organizations (approximately 60 percent) report they focus their strategy, although it may not be the best posture to execute their strategy. However, Luftman goes on to report that after formal assessment, only 6 percent of the companies were actually in this perspective. He then suggests that this means that over 50 percent of the organizations were focused inappropriately when building their strategies and action plans.

In this top-down approach the role of strategist is "leader." The leader must paint the picture of the business now and in the future, specify his desired apportionment of effort to phase and sequence the strategy to reach that future business condition and communicate the strategy throughout the company. Communication is a critical success factor for successfully executing strategy under this perspective and flow.

The human capital infrastructure is the fulcrum providing the leverage to influence (i.e., push or pull) systems (legacy or new) into alignment with the strategy. Human capital is treated as a core competency that needs to be supported by systems. Innovation exists, but it is more focused on the Operational Excellence themes associated with performance efficiency measures.

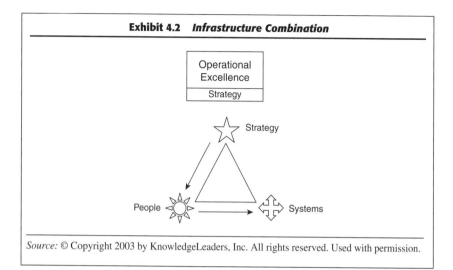

Exhibit 4.2 Infrastructure Combination

Operational
Excellence
Strategy

Strategy

People

Systems

The role of systems is to provide functional support to operations, marketing, finance and administration, and management. A systems focus is more reactive or responsive to the demands of strategy through organizational infrastructure. The objective is to meet the demands of the strategy as defined by top management. Systems support centers are treated more as cost centers. Performance measures are typically focused on performance efficiency and more traditional financial measures such as cost reduction, return on investment, return on equity, return on assets, net present value, activity-based costing, and breakeven analysis.

This approach is appealing to executives because it recognizes that systems' capabilities and peoples' competencies must be developed with strong linkages to future business needs.

Operational Excellence: Strategy to Systems to People

This is sometimes referred to as a systems transformation perspective and is pictured in Exhibit 4.3. Luftman's assessment has 20 percent of the companies formally assessing themselves falling into this category.[6] The force for change here is still top-down with strategy holding the driver dimension role, again. The area, receiving leaderships' attention to be leveraged (fulcrum dimension) is systems capital. In this flow the influenced dimension affected by systems changes is the people dimension.

In this Operational Excellence perspective, leadership's role is viewed more as that of a systems advocate. Here, business leaders analyze and push their staffs to identify how the business can better apply systems' technological advances to grow competencies and gain a competitive advantage. Business leaders must understand technological capabilities as well as the strengths and weaknesses of

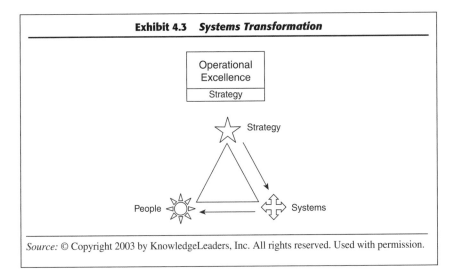

Exhibit 4.3 *Systems Transformation*

their own systems and people infrastructures. The leader is challenged with the need to choose a systems capability posture in the marketplace, while still ensuring the company's systems and people infrastructures have the absorptive capacity to assimilate the new, imported knowledge. Companies need to measure their own absorptive capacity before investing too heavily in systems that are procured to act as the fulcrum for the new strategy.

The role of the systems manager is that of a systems structural engineer who designs and manages the systems that have been defined by the business leader—the "chief strategist." The focus of systems here is that of adding value to the business not just providing cost center–type support services.

The measurable value added from this perspective and its strategy flow is in how or what systems add to the company's final product or service delivered to market, resulting in increased market share, higher returns on a new product line, increased profit though efficiencies, or increased revenues from improved asset utilization, which could then be reflected in improved growth and productivity outcome measures. Systems providers are more typically managed as a profit or investment center. In this Operational Excellence approach, a systems strategy, not a support plan, is integrated with business strategy formulation. Some systems approaches to process improvement initiatives and accelerated learning programs may have to be linked, with systems assuming a strategic fulcrum alignment role.

Product Leadership: Systems to Strategy to People

This perspective and counterclockwise strategy flow reflects a management decision to have systems and technology (current and emerging) drive new business strategies (i.e., new business lines and services) to develop a competitive advantage in the marketplace (see Exhibit 4.4). Here systems, with an emphasis on IT systems in particular, are the driver dimension. Systems and the supporting technology base will provide the force applied to shape the business strategy—the fulcrum dimension. Systems drive through strategy to push or pull the people infrastructure into alignment with a Product Leadership strategic thesis.

In this Product Leadership perspective, leadership's role is that of a business visionary or innovator. Executives must understand how to leverage systems and technology to transform their business strategies through innovative application to product and service design, development, and delivery. It is critical to ensure that senior executives are well schooled in the advances in systems technology and its potential as they develop the corporate vision of the future core business of the company.

The role of systems manager is that of a business strategy engineer and facilitator. Systems managers must play a key role in the formulation and execution of strategy. Most importantly systems managers must develop into strategists in order to be credible in formulating strategy and to be able to effectively communicate systems' value in business terms.

The system focus here is to add value to the business strategy. It is the enabler of new strategy to develop new competencies in the people infrastructure. How executives apply technology and new advanced support systems to leverage business strategy and create competitive advantage is crucial to the successful execution of strategy. The approach is grounded in finding ways to enhance systems awareness, finding new opportunities, and positioning the company to employ systems technology innovatively.

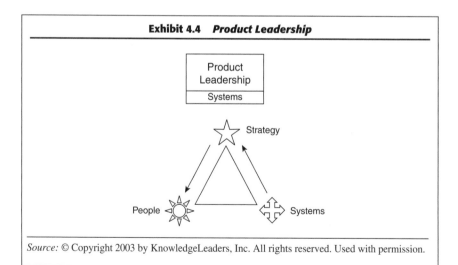

Exhibit 4.4 _Product Leadership_

Source: © Copyright 2003 by KnowledgeLeaders, Inc. All rights reserved. Used with permission.

Performance criteria for this perspective are similar to those of the Operational Excellence perspective—strategy to systems to people. This perspective is assessed on how well the application of systems to strategy directly affects a company's growth and productivity outcome measures. It is more typical of a profit or investment center operation.

This Product Leadership approach is intended to build more leverage into business strategy though systems and technology advances. Complementary intelligence-gathering tasks such as technology scans play a major part in identifying what new technologies may be applied and how these advanced systems may be applied to a business strategy and to human capital competency development. Again, a company's absorptive capacity may be the limiting factor on how effectively your company can integrate systems knowledge into driving business strategy and then push through your human capital infrastructure.

Customer Intimacy: People to Strategy to Systems

Our last strategic perspective and dimension flow analysis is our Customer Intimacy Model, shown in Exhibit 4.5. Here, the people dimension predominantly provides the force (driver dimension) on strategy, which influences systems to move into alignment. In this alignment model the direction of flow is clockwise. The fulcrum dimension is the business strategy. The affected dimension by the fulcrum is Systems. In the Customer Intimacy Dimension, the focus is on how a customer-first orientation embedded within the organizational infrastructure can carve out a strategy that leverages strategic intent against systemic structures. The strategic intent and flow of influence is to improve business processes that better

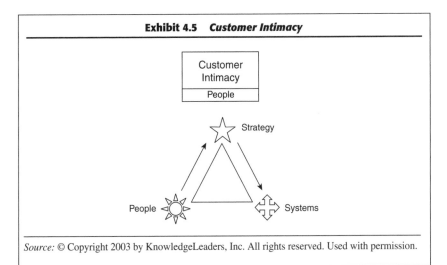

Exhibit 4.5 *Customer Intimacy*

deliver goods and services that will broaden and deepen customer relationships. Assessing how systems can improve its own embedded business processes is also part of this perspective's flow.

In this Customer Intimacy perspective, leadership's role is that of human and systems capital prioritizor. Leadership priorities for systems capabilities and human capital readiness are in direct response to customer relationship requirements. Systems are in support of areas such as internal and external customer service functional support. Since business strategy is less affected by system strategy, top leadership is less actively involved with systems strategy formulation. Leaders see systems support for internal clients as more of a business within a business relationship.

The systems manager is the executive of the systems support business. The role of systems manager is more that of a service provider than strategic planner. Strategic control is now a process for deciding how to respond to the wants and needs of internal customers who require excellent customer management processes such as relationship management and solution development to interface with the external customer. Customer management support processes might focus on systems support for the rapid acquisition of new customers. The innovation process would be motivated by the needs of targeted customers, focusing on new product development and service enhancements that contribute to better customer solutions.

Performance criteria for this perspective and driver flow are typically focused on end-user satisfaction and how systems and human capital add value to the business. For the performance measure to accurately represent the strategy, the customer outcomes, satisfaction, acquisition, retention, account share, market share, and profitability should be measured for targeted customers who, the strategic thesis claims, most appreciate the value proposition presented by the organization. People driver measures focus more on human capital metrics and their economic value added (e.g., human capital revenue, ROI human capital, human economic value added, human market value added, etc.). System support measures focus on technical areas such as systems availability, performance increases, defect reduction, and internal customer user surveys.

360-Degree SBfV Alignment Perspective Review

Essentially, when we do an alignment we want the organization to look at itself from each perspective and with different dimensions filling driver, fulcrum, and influenced roles. In the end, the company has a tightly aligned organization from all three perspectives, even though the company will lead with one, primary value proposition.

This section describes a structured method for transitioning through the SBfV Alignment Model, to assess organizational key dimensional roles and flows. The application of the SBfV Alignment Model does not stop with just assessing the components statically. How each company transitions through the SBfV Alignment Model as it executes different alignment perspectives and planning approaches is a critical piece to executing strategy.

First Phase of Alignment: Current Perspective

We begin the first transitional phase by understanding the present perspective of the company. Identify which of the three dimensions must be addressed first. That is the "center of gravity" of the business, the driver dimension. Center of gravity in military terminology refers to the "hub of all power and movement upon which everything depends."[7] The driver dimension is going to be the area that will act as the "center of gravity" of the organization. It provides the force that will be applied through the fulcrum point to affect the strategy.

After reaching consensus on the "center of gravity," next identify the fulcrum dimension. That is, the dimension that has the largest opportunity for improvement and the one that could make the biggest difference in getting you from where you are now to where you should go. This is the area that the strategic leadership team believes needs to be focused on as the "force multiplier" for strategic movement. With both the driver and fulcrum dimensions identified, the general direction of flow (clockwise or counterclockwise) that will be pursued is clear. The final point of the SBfV Alignment Model is the influence dimension

Luftman provides the following examples of how an Operational Excellence strategy with a systems orientation emerges in practice. He cites corporate cases where IBM Credit, Mutual Benefit Life Insurance (MBL), and McGraw-Hill followed a similar pattern. Each recognized the need to realign its system's pivotal role in executing its strategies through a systems approach to process improvement. IBM Credit needed to reduce the times required to develop quotes for computer processing. MBL needed to enhance the underwriting and issuing of policies. McGraw-Hill needed to differentiate its editing, marketing, and distribution of college textbooks.[8]

Each case Luftman cites began by focusing on important business processes. The fulcrum dimension for all of these companies was systems comprising interacting business processes and systemic structures that shaped organizational behaviors. The center of gravity in each of these companies was their leadership-driven strategy. Their strategies were well defined and communicated. The transition flow ran clockwise with the human capital dimension (process owners) affected by the strategic alignment. Skill sets and competencies had to align with the new systems' set of processes.

Second and Third Phases: Driver and Fulcrum

After the initial perspective and direction for the first phase of alignment is implemented, the leadership teams need to continue in the same clockwise or counterclockwise direction. In the second phase, the fulcrum dimension becomes the driver, the influenced dimension becomes the fulcrum, and the driver becomes the influenced dimension. The dimensions' order of sequencing works out the same whether the direction of flow is clockwise or counterclockwise. In the second phase, the dimension that was used to create leverage (fulcrum) becomes the driver for the next phase. This dimension should be the most current and should be reconstituted to drive the next phase. It now carries the momentum for the subsequent phase.

Continuing with the same case examples, in this second phase the systems dimension (fulcrum) becomes the driver, the organizational and people infrastructure (influenced) becomes the fulcrum, and the strategy (driver) then becomes the influenced dimension. The dimension transitions continue in the clockwise rotation. In alignment phase 3, the organizational and people dimension (fulcrum) becomes the driver, the strategy dimension (influenced) becomes the fulcrum, and the systems dimension (driver) becomes the influenced dimension. Working organizational alignment analysis through changing perspectives alters the strategic leadership approach applied, which requires continuous reassessment of mindsets, the models, and the measures of: value, strategy, strategic governance, required operational capabilities, and human capital readiness requirements. This forces leadership teams to look at the company from the three value proposition strategies—Operational Excellence, Product Leadership, and Customer Intimacy. Changing the perspectives and leadership's planning approaches enhances the ability of the company to identify innovative opportunities, while contemporaneously achieving strategic alignment.

Remember, achieving strategic alignment is not a static or one-time event. Strategic alignment is a continuous process of discovery, choice, and adaption to change.

Pincer "Push-Push-Pull" SBfV Alignments

In a perfect world, the four basic alignment perspectives and driver combinations (see Exhibit 4.6) are more effective when synergy is created through structured push-pull synchronization within the SBfV Alignment Model. Each of the four alignment perspectives becomes more effective when leadership establishes push and pull structures into each of the alignment models. This is done when the driver dimension pushes out to the other SBfV alignment dimensions (fulcrum and influenced) and the influenced dimension concurrently exerts a pull on the fulcrum in the direction of strategic intent.

Exhibit 4.6   *Push-Push-Pull Fulcrum*

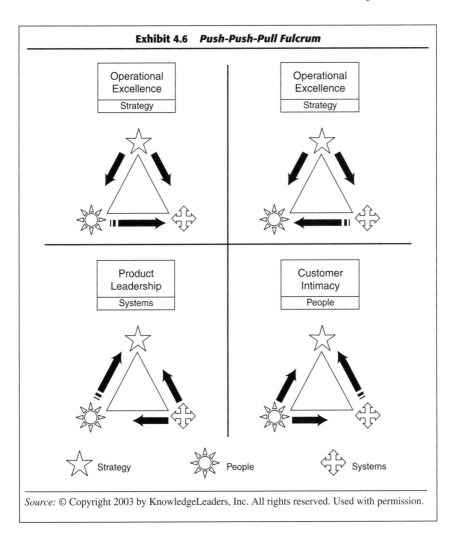

Again, we begin this alignment process by assessing the present perspective of the organization—Operational Excellence, Product Leadership, Customer Intimacy—and the "center of gravity" of the business: strategy, systems, or people.

Operational Excellence: Driver = Strategy, Fulcrum = People, Influenced = Systems

In this pincer alignment model, strategy in the driver role pushes out to both the fulcrum (people) and the influenced (systems) dimension. This force can be executed by having both people and systems mapped and fit directly to strategy. Then, you use systemic structures to pull the people dimension into closer alignment with strategic intent through functional integration of people to systems. So, in the pincher alignment you are concurrently and consistently applying strategic fit and functional integration to achieve strategic alignment. See Exhibit 4.7 as an example.

Operational Excellence: Driver = Strategy, Fulcrum = Systems,
Influenced = People

Again, strategy, as driver, pushes out to both the fulcrum (systems) and the influenced (people) dimension. This is still executed by having both people and systems mapped and fit directly to strategy. But, in this pincer movement we use people or organizational infrastructure to pull systems into closer alignment with strategic intent through functional integration of systems support to people readiness requirements. Again, you are concurrently applying strategic fit and functional integration to achieve strategic alignment. See Exhibit 4.8 as an example. This is accomplished through prioritization matrices, performance measures, strategic apportionments, and tactical resource allocations that will be introduced later in this chapter.

Product Leadership: Driver = Systems, Fulcrum = People,
Influenced = Strategy

In this and the next pincer alignment, strategy is no longer the driver. Here, the model supports a less deliberate and more emergent mode of formulating strategy.

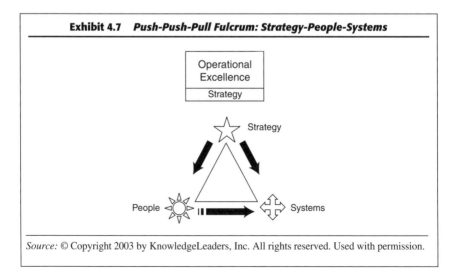

Exhibit 4.7   *Push-Push-Pull Fulcrum: Strategy-People-Systems*

Operational Excellence

Strategy

Strategy

People   Systems

Source: © Copyright 2003 by KnowledgeLeaders, Inc. All rights reserved. Used with permission.

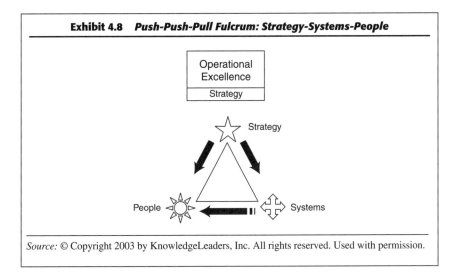

Exhibit 4.8   Push-Push-Pull Fulcrum: Strategy-Systems-People

Under this alignment, systems acts as the driver, which is then used to push out to shape both the peoples' competency levels and the strategy itself—product leadership. Human capital acts as the fulcrum (force multiplier), and strategy is the influenced dimension (see Exhibit 4.9). But in this pincer movement we use the strategic fit of human capital to strategy to pull competencies into closer alignment with strategic intent. And, we use a functional mapping of systems to people to

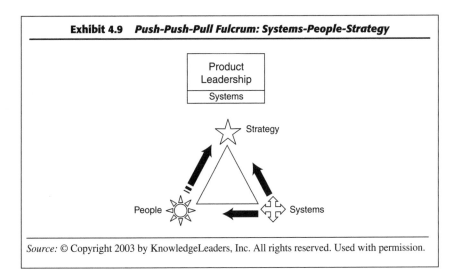

Exhibit 4.9   Push-Push-Pull Fulcrum: Systems-People-Strategy

push competency levels higher in order to support a more technically innovative, less deliberate strategy.

Customer Intimacy: Driver = People, Fulcrum = Systems, Influenced = Strategy

Again, in this alignment strategy is not the driver. This model also supports a less deliberate and more emergent mode of formulating strategy (see Exhibit 4.10). Under this alignment, people act as the driver that is then used to push out, to shape, both the systems' required operational capabilities and the strategy itself—customer intimacy. System capital acts as the fulcrum (force multiplier), and strategy is the influenced dimension. Moreover, in this pincer movement we use the strategic fit of systems capital to strategy to pull systems requirement into closer alignment with strategic intent. Concurrently, we use a functional mapping of people to systems to push systems' capabilities and reliability levels higher in order to support a strategy focused on establishing excellent customer relationships supported by technological innovations.

The Economic Costs of Strategic Misalignment

The principles that guide corporate economics do not change. The collapse of the dot.coms supports this thesis. Strategy evolves within the context and realities of

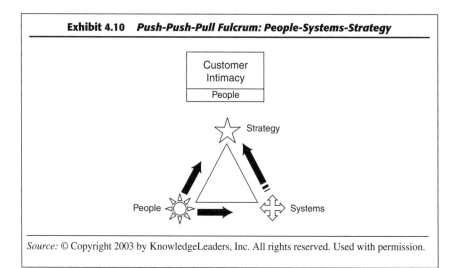

Exhibit 4.10   Push-Push-Pull Fulcrum: People-Systems-Strategy

Source: © Copyright 2003 by KnowledgeLeaders, Inc. All rights reserved. Used with permission.

the corporate environment. Strategy aligns principles with vision to create value. However, today we recognize a strategy environment misalignment. The market, values leadership's ability to execute strategy by combining tangible and intangible assets in cause-and-effect linkages to achieve economic and political goals. The cause-and-effect linkages connect the value drivers that best correlate with achieving desired outcomes. This drives investment to companies able to communicate this value-building ability through financial communiqués to the market. And yet, we still are unable to observe effective strategy execution for sustaining optimal revenue and value growth in an uncertain environment.

Exhibit 4.11 shows an example of strategic misalignment. Compare this with Exhibit 4.12, which shows how a company's strategy can be realigned for effective execution and optimal growth.

Absorptive Capacity

The strategic alignment of people and systems yields measurable organizational core competencies. It also determines the "absorptive capacity" level of your organization.

Absorptive capacity is defined as the ability of a firm to recognize the value of new, external information, assimilate it, and apply it to commercial ends. Absorptive capacity works both at the people and the systems level. At the people level, the accumulation of prior knowledge enhances the ability to acquire new knowledge. Similarly, the diversity of prior knowledge facilitates the generation of novel associations and linkages and helps one deal with uncertainty. Absorptive capacity at the systems level is shaped by organizational structure in conjunction with the absorptive capacity at the individual level.

The effect of absorptive capacity is cumulative, since it enhances the company's ability to assimilate and exploit new knowledge and to evaluate the importance of new technological advances.

A low level of absorptive capacity may hinder your company's appreciation of emerging new technologies and opportunities and cause it to be more reactive. A high level of absorptive capacity will help your company be more proactive and exploit emerging new technologies and market opportunities.

Absorptive capacity is highest in your areas of core competencies. We call these areas dimensions of absorptive capacity. Since organizational absorptive capacity is a function of prior knowledge, you can increase absorptive capacity by increasing your resource allocation in your chosen areas of core competencies. This is another reason why it is important for SBfV to identify your company's core competencies and strategize how you will enhance them and leverage them.

Exhibit 4.11 *Strategy, Systems, People Misalignment*

Strategic Resource Alignment—200 Employee Business Unit

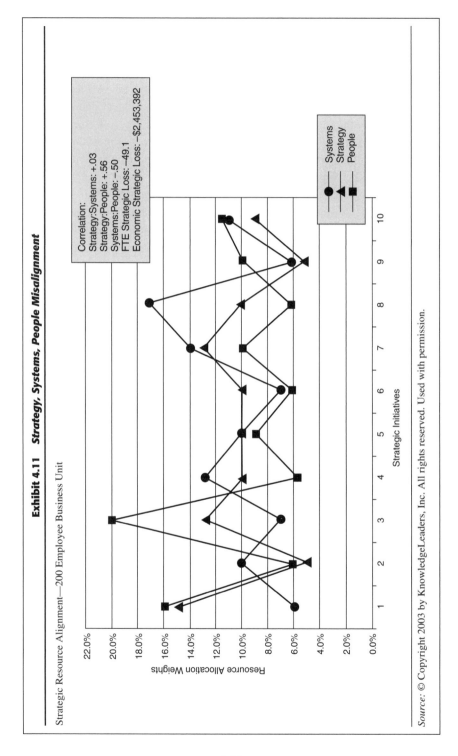

Correlation:
Strategy:Systems: +.03
Strategy:People: +.56
Systems:People: −.50
FTE Strategic Loss: −49.1
Economic Strategic Loss: −$2,453,392

Systems
Strategy
People

Resource Allocation Weights

Strategic Initiatives

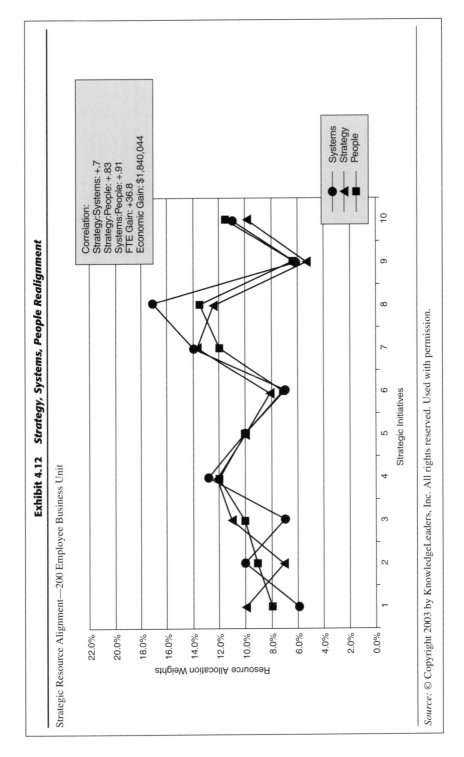

Exhibit 4.12 Strategy, Systems, People Realignment

Strategic Resource Alignment—200 Employee Business Unit

Correlation:
Strategy:Systems: +.7
Strategy:People: +.83
Systems:People: +.91
FTE Gain: +36.8
Economic Gain: $1,840,044

Resource Allocation Weights

Strategic Initiatives

Systems
Strategy
People

The Costs of Misalignment

Return on Strategic Effectiveness

So how is your ROSE today? SBfV's measure of the Value State is used to track the readiness status of your tangible and intangible assets. SBfV clearly articulates your strategy so that you are able to track the readiness of your assets to support your strategy. SBfV's Value State for intangibles is analogous to liquidity. The higher the Value State the faster the intangible assets can be converted into tangible assets. Just as the balance sheet is a periodic report that describes the status of financial assets, SBfV's Value State reporting performs the same function for intangible inputs and tangible outputs. The SBfV Value Effectiveness Measure provides you with the level of readiness of each identified value driver required to support your strategy. SBfV's Value State report is built on the assumption that the company's ability to execute strategy is its primary source of value. It provides a snapshot, at a given point in time, of the status of human capital relative to the requirements to successfully execute strategy.

The right people end up in the right jobs at the right time when strategically relevant information about human capital is monitored constantly and leaders know the people, how they work together, and whether they deliver key results. If your company has the right people with the right stuff working on the right activities, your strategies and systems will be aligned and in sync with the realities of the marketplace, changing economic environments, and ahead of your competition. Your organization will be maximizing its value-creating potential.

NOTES

1. Bob Thompson, "Bumbling Mavericks Clobbered," *Columbia Daily Tribune* (August 16, 2003).
2. Ernst & Young, *Measures That Matter*™ (Boston: Ernst & Young, 1998), p. 9.
3. Carl Von Clausewitz, *On War*, edited and translated by Michael Howard and Peter Paret (Princeton: Princeton University Press, 1976), pp. 177–178.
4. Research by Leonard Nakamura, Federal Reserve Bank of Philadelphia presented at the 4th Intangibles Conference, "What Is the U.S. Gross Investment in Intangibles? (At Least) One Trillion Dollars a Year!" Stern School of Business, New York University, May 17–18, 2001.
5. Jerry N. Luftman, *Competing in the Information Age* (New York: Oxford University Press, 1996). p. 46
6. *Ibid.* p. 53
7. Carl Von Clausewitz, *On War*, edited and translated by Michael Howard and Peter Paret (Princeton: Princeton University Press, 1976), 177–178.
8. Jerry N. Luftman, *Competing in the Information Age* (New York: Oxford University Press, 1996). p. 61.

Benchmark and Monitor Return on Strategy Execution

BENCHMARK AND MONITOR RETURN ON STRATEGY EXECUTION

We have now taken you through the SBfV Process by:

- Determining your company's Current State on a qualitative and quantitative basis.
- Deciding where you want the company to go in the Future State.
- Developing a workable strategy and executing it using strategic benchmarking keys, which focus is then cascaded through the company by following the paths of critical success factors and key performance indicators.
- Aligning your company's systems and people to the defined strategy so that everyone is singing out of the same book.

But, to date ourselves: Where's the beef? What does all this work mean and how does it improve your Company's value?

The key to answering these questions lies in the SBfV Scorecard. It is the device that captures the SBfV Framework (the elements of your company). It converts the various SBfV strategy maps (the cause and effect relationships of your company's elements) into a readable, timely, and workable format. Finally it provides you with the Return on Strategic Effectiveness (ROSE) (see Exhibit 5.1) and allows you to focus on accountability and corrective action. The SBfV Process is a continuous process, a loop, much as your business process is continuous . . . or payday stops.

Scorecards are a tool that can take many forms. They can be simple or complex, although we recommend a simple design at the start of their use in most com-

Exhibit 5.1 ROSE Framework Strategy Map

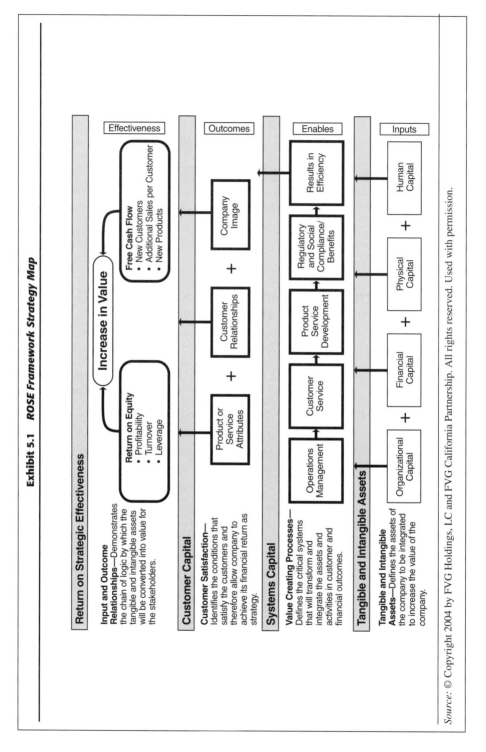

panies. They can include graphics, dashboards (very popular now), and a variety of other cosmetic designs. Many times, they are forced onto one page whereas other designs require the use of multiple pages. SBfV designed scorecards for owners or senior managers that will generally consist of at least two pages with the Mobley Matrix for the current accounting period and the year-to-day period requiring a page of their own.

To describe the effectiveness and flexibility of the scorecard, we want to review the SBfV Framework, but this time present it in a different format, more like a traditional flowchart. The beauty of maps is their flexibility and effectiveness of communication. Exhibit 5.2 presents the framework in a top-down format.

Now here is the key to Scorecards: Turn the above "map" on its ear. That's right, turn it 90 degrees to the left. Now you have a process flow going left to right.

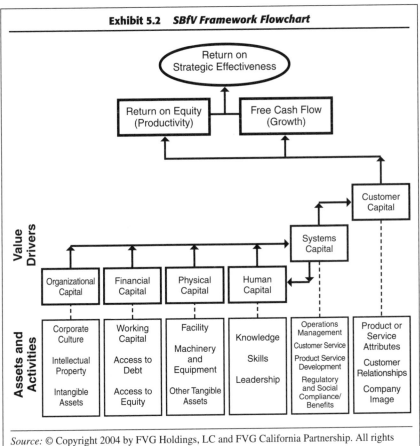

Exhibit 5.2 *SBfV Framework Flowchart*

Source: © Copyright 2004 by FVG Holdings, LC and FVG California Partnership. All rights reserved. Used with permission.

The company's strategy and goals (Productivity and Growth) are on the left. These cascade into the Six Types of Capital, which constitute every company. These goals then feed "down" to the various activities necessary to execute the processes to meet the goals.

Retail Business Strategic Transformation Story

Let us build a scorecard for a retail store whose owners want to install a bar code reader at the point of sale. Remember, scorecards are extremely flexible and no two are the same. The beauty of the scorecard is that it presents a simple overview of a project or projects being implemented in a disciplined manner reflected through the company's processes. In this example, our ROSE (return on equity, profitability, asset turnover, leverage, and free cash flow) will be affected by the addition to assets and debt due to the purchase of the equipment. From SBfV's Five Dimensions of Value, the bar code project is likely to improve employee productivity. The critical success factors are accuracy and ease of checkout, for both the customer and the clerk. As we go through the Customer Capital level, customer satisfaction will be affected by the time portion of product attributes for two reasons: checkout time should be reduced by, say, 60 seconds and accuracy at checkout should be improved. The value-creating process at the Systems Level of Capital, specifically the operations and knowledge management systems, will be enhanced because the items packaged in the store will have to be labeled with bar codes. All items bought from outside vendors will be purchased on the condition of being labeled with bar codes. Within the Assets and Activities, financial capital, specifically access to debt, will have a date certain for financing approval. Under Physical Capital, the bar code equipment will need to be purchased and installed. Under Human Capital, management and clerks will need specialized training and skills.

Performance measures will be established with benchmarks and targets. Specific activities will be defined to accomplish the project with supporting action plans and budgeting.

Now, compare this narrative with the clarity and conciseness of Exhibit 5.3. The associated map delineating cause and effect relationships for this project is in Exhibit 5.4.

This is obviously a simple example to demonstrate the use of the scorecard within the SBfV Framework. A more complex example, below the ROE and Mobley Matrix level, relating to developing an improved relationship with the stores' customers (customer intimacy) as shown in Exhibits 5.5 and 5.6.

Finally, we demonstrate two strategy maps with the strategy of developing operational excellence in the public sector in Exhibit 5.7, and in the information technology (IT) division in Exhibit 5.8.

Exhibit 5.3 Example Bar Code Project Scorecard

Critical Success Factors	Assets and Activities	Performance Measures	Benchmarks	
			Target	Actual
Accuracy and ease of check-out	Product attribute (time)	• Reduce checkout time by 60 seconds	210 sec.	270 sec.
		• Improve accuracy at checkout	99.5%	96%
	Operations and knowledge management systems	• Bar code items packaged in store	100%	0%
	Knowledge skills	• Train management and clerks	Date Specific	
	Equipment	• Purchase and install bar code system	Date Specific	
	Access to debt	• Arrange financing within 2 months	Date Specific	

Customer Capital — Systems Capital — Human Capital — Physical Capital — Financial Capital — Organizational Capital

Free Cash Flow (Growth): • Revenue • Expenses

Return on Equity (Productivity): • Profitability • Asset Turnover • Leverage

Return on Strategic Effectiveness

Exhibit 5.4   Retail Store Project: Bar Code Readers

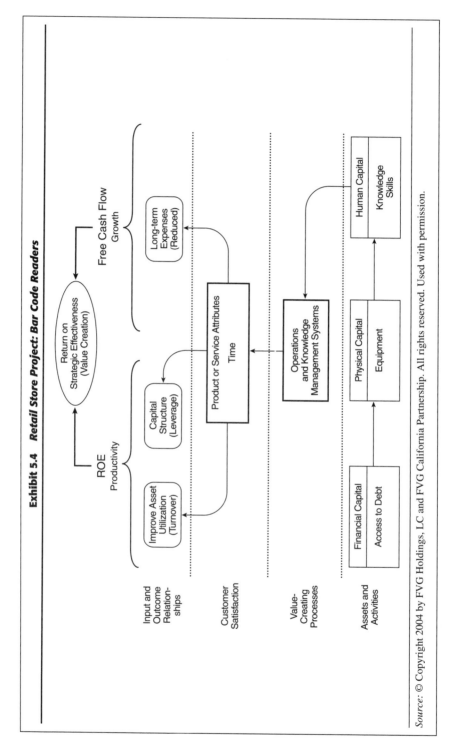

Exhibit 5.5 Retail (For Profit) Company's "ROSE" Map (Customer Intimacy)

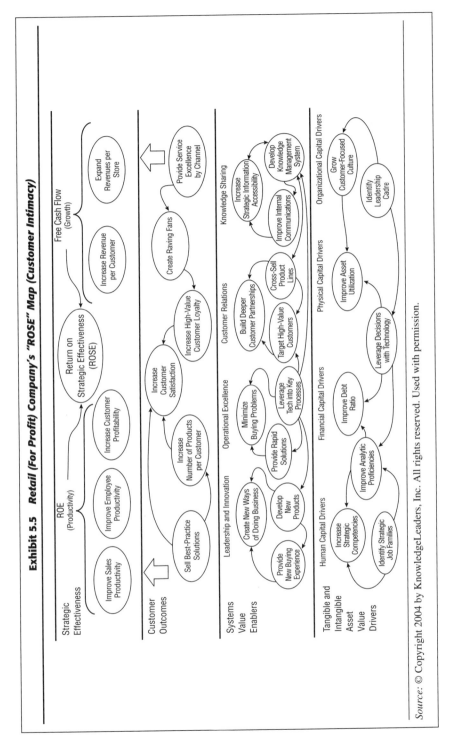

Exhibit 5.6 Retail (For-Profit) Company's "ROSE" Scorecard (Customer Intimacy)

Strategic Objectives	Performance Measures	Benchmarks	
		Target	Actual
Return on Strategic Effectiveness			
Productivity			
Improve Sales Productivity	Cost of Sales	62%	64%
Improve Employee Productivity	Profit per Employee	(+) 4%	3%
Increase Customer Profitability	Profit per Customer	(+)15%	UNKN
Growth			
Increase Revenue per Customer	Share of Wallet	50%	35%
Expand Revenue per Store	Percent Increase Average Annual Revenue per Store	(+) 10%	(+) 5%
Customer			
Increase Customer Satisfaction	Percent Customers Highly Satisfied	90%	75%
Sell Best-Practice Solutions	Percent Jointly Developed Product Lines	45%`	25%
Increase Number of Products per Customer	Number of Products per Customer	4	2
Increase High-Value Customer Loyalty	High-Value Customer Retention Percent	80%	62.5%
Create Raving Fans	Percent of Business from Customer Referrals	15%	8%
Provide Service Excellence per Channel	Service Performance Data by Channel	7	5.5
Systems Value Enablers			
Leadership and Innovation			
Create New Ways of Doing Business	Revenue Growth from New Business	(+) 12.5%	(+) 7%
Provide New Buying Experience	Customer Buying Experience Ratings	8	6.5
Develop New Products	Number of New Products Launched or Commercialized	4	2
Operational Excellence			
Minimize Buying Problems	Number of Complaints Trend per Store	(−) 12%	(+) 2.5%

Provide Rapid Solutions	Average Time to Resolve Disputes	(−) 25%	up 12%
Leverage Technology into Key Processes	Number of Key Processes Automated	50%	35%
Customer Relations			
Build Deeper Customer Relations	Number of Communications with High-Value Customer	(+) 10%	NA
Target High-Value Customers	Number of Strategic Accounts	(+) 15%	NA
Cross-Sell Product Lines	Cross-sell Ratio	(+) 3%	UNKN
Knowledge Sharing			
Increase Strategic Information Accessibility	Strategic Information Portfolio Readiness	90%	75%
Improve Internal Communications	Percent of Staff Using Knowledge Sharing Channels	80%	0%
Develop Knowledge Management System	Best-practice Sharing (Number of KMS hits/employee)	25/wk	0/wk
Tangible and Intangible Assets Value Drivers			
Human Capital Drivers			
Increase Strategic Competencies	Human Capital Readiness Index	90%	60%
Identify Strategic Job Families	Percent of Strategic Jobs Profiled and Filled	90%	75%
Improve Analytic Proficiencies	Percent of Medium level Analytically Profiled Jobs	50%	40%
Financial Capital Drivers			
Improve Debt Ratio	Debt Ratio	55%	66%
Leverage Decisions with Technology	Financial Capital Readiness Index	85%	65%
Physical Capital Drivers			
Improve Asset Utilization	Annual Revenue per Square Foot	(+) 10%	6.5%
Leverage Decisions with Technology	Physical Capital Readiness Index	90%	75%
Organization Capital Drivers			
Grow Customer-focused Culture	Customer Survey	(+) 15%	UNKN
Identify Leadership Cadre	Leadership Competency Index	80%	65%

Note: Each supporting activity would be supported by a detailed action plan with a specific project leader (champion).

Source: © Copyright 2004 by KnowledgeLeaders, Inc. All rights reserved. Used with permission.

Exhibit 5.7   Public Sector (Not-for-Profit) Company's "ROSE" Map (Operational Excellence)

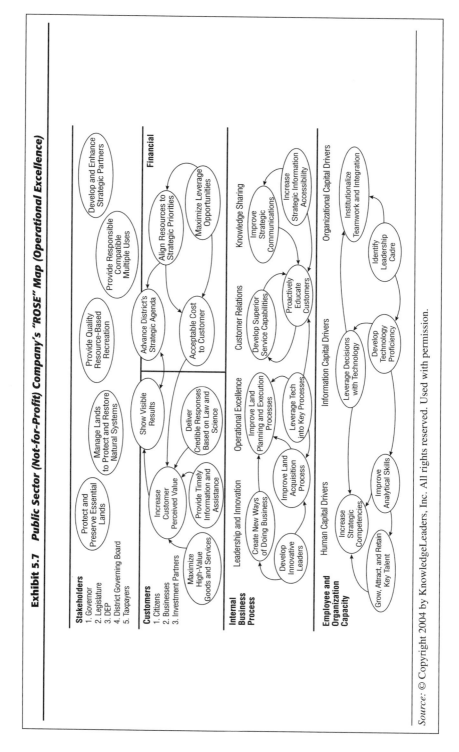

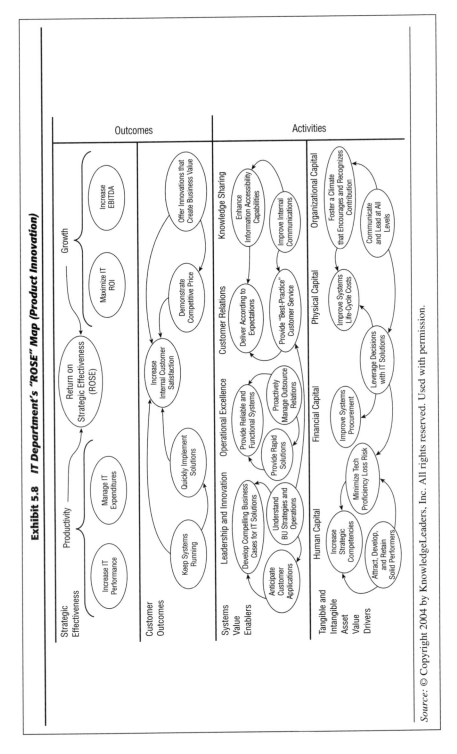

Exhibit 5.8   IT Department's "ROSE" Map (Product Innovation)

Source: © Copyright 2004 by KnowledgeLeaders, Inc. All rights reserved. Used with permission.

Exhibit 5.9 Mobley Matrix

Sample Widget Manufacturing Company
Mobley Matrix
For the Year
($000)

Beginning Balance sheet 12/31/XXXX		Income Statement		Cash Flow Statement		Ending Balance Sheet 12/31/XXXX	
Cash	$ 25			Cash Increase (Decrease)	$(23)	Cash	$ 2
Accounts Receivable	35	Sales	$500	Collections	475	Accounts Receivable	60
Inventory	75	Cost of Goods Sold	310	Inventory Paid	340	Inventory	105
Other Operating Assets	10			Prepayments	10	Other Operating Assets	0
Notes Receivable	0			Lend/Receive	0	Notes Receivable	0
Gross Fixed Assets	100			Fixed Asset Investment	20	Gross Fixed Assets	120
Accumulated Depreciation	30	Depreciation Expense	10			Accumulated Depreciation	40
Net Fixed Assets	70					Net Fixed Assets	80
Other Investments	30	Intangible Amortization	2	Other Investment	0	Other Investments	28
Total Assets	$ 245					Total Assets	$ 275
Accounts Payable	$20	Marketing, Selling, G&A Exp.	155	Expense Paid	143	Accounts Payable	$ 32
Debt	15			Borrow/Payback	5	Debt	20
Other Operating Liabilities	0	Interest & Other Expense	1	Interest & Other Expense Paid	1	Other Operating Liabilities	0
Income Taxes Due	5	Income Tax Expense	6	Income Taxes Paid	8	Income Taxes Due	3
Non-operating Liabilities	0	Non-operating Expense	0	Non-operating Expense Paid	0	Non-operating Liabilities	0
Stock	100			Paid-In	0	Stock	100
Retained Earnings	105	Net Profit	16	Dividend & Other Payouts	1	Retained Earnings	120
Total Liabilities & Equity	$ 245			Free Cash Flow	$(22)	Total Liabilities & Equity	$ 275

Note: "Prepayments" are a source of funds that are expensed under "Expense Paid".
Source: © Copyright 2004 jointly owned by Chris Mobley, Mobley Matrix International, Inc., and Chuck Kremer.

CLOSING

This book, by design, is a brief overview of the SBfV Process, one that is unique in the literature today but not unique to day-to-day owners and managers. We have introduced six levels of capital common to all businesses (see Exhibit 5.1) that must be managed by its people using systems consistent with the company's strategy. SBfV focuses on tangible as well as intangible assets. Importantly, SBfV is able to identify and measure gaps in hard performance through the Mobley Matrix cash flow analysis (Exhibit 5.9) and the DuPont formula's ROE shortfalls, as well as gaps in soft performance (groups of people marching to a different drummer). By identifying, measuring, and managing these hard and soft gaps, the company is able to bring strategy, systems, and people into alignment, which in turn maximizes value (see Exhibit 5.10).

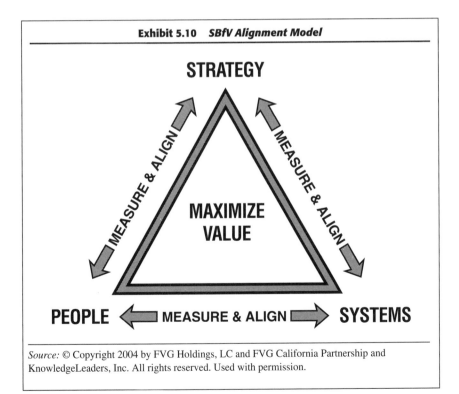

Exhibit 5.10   *SBfV Alignment Model*

STRATEGY

MEASURE & ALIGN

MEASURE & ALIGN

MAXIMIZE VALUE

PEOPLE ⟵ MEASURE & ALIGN ⟶ SYSTEMS

Source: © Copyright 2004 by FVG Holdings, LC and FVG California Partnership and KnowledgeLeaders, Inc. All rights reserved. Used with permission.

APPENDIX:

Websites of Interest

The following list of websites represents only a fraction of all of those on the WorldWide Web that relate to performance measurement and value creation. These are just a few that we have come across for various reasons that may be of interest to the reader.

Sites Related to the Authors:
The Financial Valuation Group
www.fvginternational.com
The Financial Valuation Group is one of the leading business valuation, consulting, and litigation service firms that provides services throughout the United States and Latin America.
Strategic Benchmarking for Value
www.strategicbenchmarking.com
Provides an overview of the Strategic Benchmarking for Value process and model, and an interactive playground that allows management to begin a review of the company's state of development and the effectiveness of its workforce.
Mentor Plus
www.mentorplus.com
Mentor Plus provides leading edge business development tools and support to help you build the business your customers really want.

Other sites, in no particular order:
Matt H. Evans, CPA, CMA, CFM: Creating Value through Excellence in Financial Management
www.exinfm.com/free_spreadsheets.html
You can easily learn about "real" finance by tapping into some of the resources offered on this website.
Ernst & Young
www.ey.com/global/content.nsf/uk/cf_-_Library_-_MTM
"Measures that Matter™," an outside-in perspective on shareholder value recognition, includes:
- Contents—including foreword
- Executive Summary
- The shareholder value model has changed

- Nonfinancial performance counts
- Companies need to recognize their nonfinancial performance

PricewaterhouseCoopers

*www.pwcglobal.com/extweb/newcoatwork.nsf/docid/770B39BC7378980980256DA
D0046733F*

"Outperformance: Delivering Better Returns Over the Long Term." This article demonstrates the importance of the development of "shareholder value" as a key measure of corporate performance.

Stern Stewart & Company

www.sternstewart.com/evaabout/whatis.php

Guides client companies through the implementation of a complete EVA-based financial management and incentive compensation system.

Malaspina University–College

http://planning.mala.bc.ca/primer/primer.asp?title=definition7&section=2)

SWOT analysis is a general technique that can find suitable applications across diverse management functions and activities. It is particularly appropriate to the early stages of strategic and marketing planning.

CMA Management

www.managementmag.com.

CMA Management is a dynamic business magazine designed to help senior management professionals make informed decisions and give them a strategic advantage.

Competitive Edge

www.competitiveedge.com/

Competitive Edge has helped scores of organizations and departments "go for the gold" by focusing their strategic direction through scientific and systematic customer input.

Mind Tools

www.mindtools.com/

Mind Tools outlines important life and career skills in easy to understand language. These are supported by simple examples and exercises that expand and reinforce your understanding.

Pilot Software

www.pilotsoftware.com

Pilot provides operational performance management that enables organizations to rapidly achieve objectives by aligning execution with strategy.

Business Performance Improvement Resource (BPIR)

www.bpir.com

The BPIR is one of a number of initiatives that is managed by the Centre for Organisational Excellence Research (COER), which exists to help organizations improve their performance through acquiring, sharing, and applying knowledge relating to organizational excellence.

CODA: Financial Intelligence

www.coda.com

CODA is a leading global provider of award-winning accounting and procurement systems, versatile financial analysis tools, and consultancy services that help users streamline and automate their finance processes.

Value Based Management.net

www.valuebasedmanagement.net

Management services on value creation, managing for value, and valuation.

Knowledge@Wharton, The Wharton School, University of PA

http://knowledge.wharton.upenn.edu

Knowledge@Wharton is a bi-weekly online resource that offers the latest business insights, information, and research from a variety of sources.

META Group

www.metagroup.com

META Group is a leading provider of information technology research, advisory services, and strategic consulting.

The Grove Consultants International

www.grove.com

The Grove Consultants International is a process-consulting firm committed to advancing the art and practice of collaboration.

DM Review

www.dmreview.com

DM Review is recognized as the premier business intelligence, analytics, and data warehousing publication.

Department of Trade and Industry (U.K.)

www.dti.gov.uk

We help people and companies become more productive by promoting enterprise, innovation, and creativity.

Decision Point Solutions, LLC

www.decisionpoint.la

Specializing in performance measurement systems for Strategic Benchmarking for Value, Sarbanes-Oxley compliance and monitoring, and strategy implementations.

Index

189

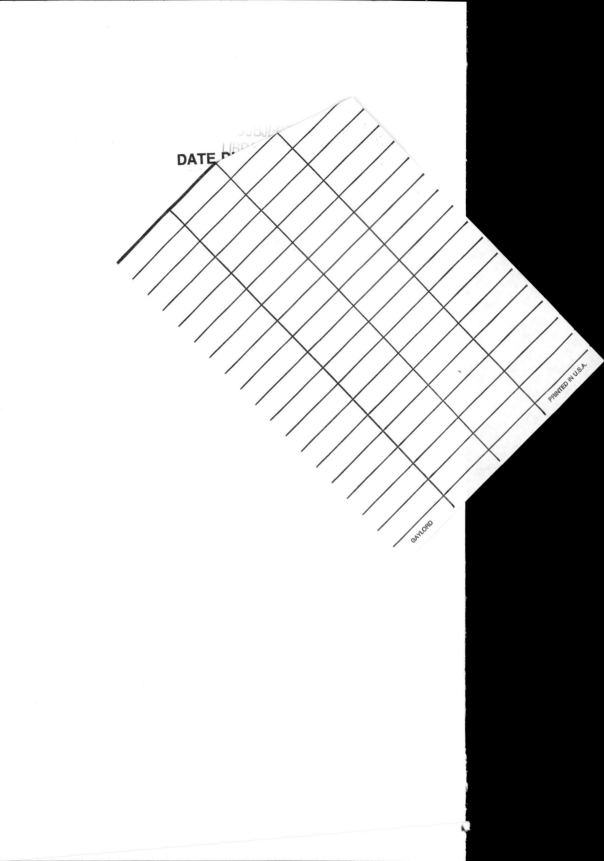

DATE D

PRINTED IN U.S.A.

GAYLORD